# The World Bank's Lending
# in South Asia

*Brookings Occasional Papers*

# The World Bank's Lending in South Asia

S. GUHAN

**THE BROOKINGS INSTITUTION**
Washington, D.C.

*Brookings Occasional Papers*

THE BROOKINGS INSTITUTION is a private nonprofit organization devoted to research, education, and publication on important issues of domestic and foreign policy. Its principal purpose is to bring knowledge to bear on the major policy problems facing the American people.

On occasion Brookings publishes research papers that warrant immediate circulation as contributions to the public debate on current policy issues. Because of the speed of their production, these Occasional Papers are not subjected to all of the formal review and verification procedures established for the Institution's research publications, and they may be revised at a later date. As in all Brookings publications, the judgments, conclusions, and recommendations presented in the Papers are solely those of the authors and should not be attributed to the trustees, officers, or other staff members of the Institution.

## Acknowledgments

I am indebted to John P. Lewis, Devesh Kapur, Richard Webb, Michael Baxter, Robert Cassen, William Gilmartin, Paul Isenman, Jochen Kraske, Attila Karaosmangolu, Robert Picciotto, Robert Planfil, Frances Plunkett, Ashok Seth, Steve Talbot, Heinz Vergin, Mervyn Weiner, and Oktay Yenal for saving me from errors of fact and judgment. They have tried their best. Particular thanks are due to John Lewis and Devesh Kapur for continued advice and interaction. Laura Powell and Karen Semkow in Washington and Maheswari in Madras have provided valuable support.

## Introduction

From their founding through the end of fiscal year 1990 the World Bank and its affiliate the International Development Association (IDA) funded 719 project operations in the seven countries of South Asia, for a total of more than $50 billion, spread over more than twenty sectors and subsectors.[1] The region contains some of the oldest and largest borrowers of the World Bank Group and includes India, its largest single borrower. Containing a fifth of the world's population and perhaps three-quarters of its absolute poor, South Asia has been, and will continue to be, a prime theater of involvement for the Bank.[2]

The scope of this paper is confined to the project lending operations of the Bank in South Asia and needs to be situated in the wider context of Bank-borrower relationships that will be discussed in a forthcoming history of the World Bank. It must also be selective in its treatment of major topics, given the volume, scope, and diversity of the Bank's project lending. Moreover, whereas this review is confined to a window of time, the Bank is a continually evolving organization, and therefore some of the judgments made here are likely to have only a transient validity. Despite these limitations, a study of what the Bank has attempted, achieved, and failed to achieve in the 1970s and 1980s should be of special interest for at least two reasons. First, these two decades witnessed a phenomenal growth and diversification in project lending, making them a particularly active and interesting period. Second, the 1970s and 1980s may also prove to have been a watershed, since the coming decades in South Asia are likely to see a slowdown in the growth of overall lending levels as well as a shift toward nonproject, adjustment lending.

The paper is organized as follows. The first section sets out the development context in South Asia by way of background. The second discusses the important characteristics of project lending in the region. The third reviews lending strategies, the policy dialogue, and project impact in terms of major sectors and borrowers. The concluding section puts together an overall assessment of the Bank's project lending experience over the two decades.

1

## South Asia: The Development Context

The countries of South Asia, despite important differences, share several characteristics that distinguish them as a region. The main land mass of South Asia is marked off from the rest of the continent by the deserts of Balochistan in the northwest, the Himalayan ranges in the wide middle, and the thick jungles of northeastern India and Myanmar in the east. The Indus River basin straddles Pakistan and India, while the Ganges and the Brahmaputra flow through India and Bangladesh.

The South Asian countries are reasonably well endowed with minerals and with fuel resources for energy development. Hydroelectric resources are important for power generation in India, Pakistan, and Sri Lanka, and there is massive untapped potential in Nepal. There is considerable scope for irrigation in all the major countries of the region. Except from the rivers fed by Himalayan snowmelt, irrigation depends directly on rain or on rain-fed rivers or on groundwater recharged by rain and river flows. The combination of snowmelt and rain in the summer months often leads to heavy flooding in the north and northeast of the subcontinent, Bangladesh being particularly vulnerable. Droughts are equally common, and it is not unusual for different parts of the region to be in the grip of floods and drought at the same time. Cyclonic storms in the Bay of Bengal periodically cause heavy damage to lives, crops, homes, and property in Bangladesh and along the eastern coast of India. Although seismic activity is not frequent, serious earthquakes have occurred in Nepal, in northern India and Pakistan, and most recently in central India. Soil waterlogging and salinity caused by the formation of alkaline pans are major problems in Pakistan.

### Demographics

The South Asian population of nearly 1.1 billion as of mid-1991 is shared very unequally among the countries in the region (table 1). India, the second most populous country in the world, accounts for more than three-quarters of the region's total, with a current population of about 850 million. Far behind

2

but next in size come Bangladesh and Pakistan, with populations of around 110 million each, while Nepal and Sri Lanka each have populations of a little less than 20 million. Bhutan (1.4 million) and Maldives (0.2 million) are tiny. Since 1960 annual population growth in the region has been around 2.3 percent, with a marginal slackening to 2.2 percent in the 1980s. There is considerable variation among the major South Asian countries in population growth rates and their determinants. India, growing by 2.1 percent per year between 1980 and 1990, is still adding about 18 million every year to its numbers. Current annual growth rates are also high in three of the other countries: 3.1 percent in Pakistan, 2.1 percent in Bangladesh, and 2.6 percent in Nepal. Sri Lanka has, in contrast, achieved an impressive demographic transition, bringing down birth and death rates to 20 and 6 per 1,000, respectively, and its current growth rate to 1.4 percent per year.

With one-fifth of the world's population, South Asia occupies barely 4 percent of global land area; accordingly, population densities are very high. The level and growth of urbanization, however, have so far remained low. Even in India and Pakistan, which are the most urbanized, about 70 percent of the people live in rural areas. City sizes have grown in absolute numbers, however, and increasingly the provision of urban services has emerged as a major problem and an expensive one. The large absolute sizes and high densities of population in South Asia have many consequences and implications for development: there is intense pressure on the environment; agricultural holdings are small and fragmented; the cost of providing education, health, and other basic services is high; and urban congestion is a serious problem.

### Gross National Product

The South Asian countries are all classified by the World Bank as low-income, and four of them—Bangladesh, Nepal, Bhutan, and Maldives—are classified as least developed. The region as a whole recorded an average annual real GNP growth of 4.3 percent in the 1960s, which declined to 3.5 percent in the 1970s but accelerated to over 5 percent in the 1980s. South Asia's growth performance is doubtless modest, but it has been sustained and there are some hopeful signs of acceleration. Also, the region's recent performance is impressive in that it represents a break from that of the colonial period before the 1950s, when long-term growth was barely 1 percent per year, agricultural growth stagnated, and per capita real incomes were stationary despite low (around 1 percent) population growth.[3]

There are fairly wide variations in growth performance, overall and per

Table 1. Population Characteristics for Seven South Asian Countries, Selected Periods, 1980–91

| Indicator | India | Pakistan | Bangladesh | Sri Lanka | Nepal | Bhutan | Maldives |
|---|---|---|---|---|---|---|---|
| Population, 1990 (millions) | 850.0 | 112.0 | 107.0 | 17.0 | 18.9 | 1.4 | 0.2 |
| Population density, 1991 (persons per square kilometer) | 253.0 | 137.0 | 725.0 | 256.0 | 131.0 | 30.0 | 693.0 |
| Average annual growth of population, 1980–90 (percent) | 2.1 | 3.1 | 2.1 | 1.4 | 2.6 | 2.2 | 3.2 |
| Urban share of total population, 1990 (percent) | 27.0 | 32.0 | 16.4 | 21.4 | 9.6 | 5.2 | 29.4 |
| Average annual growth of urban population, 1980–90 (percent) | 3.6 | 4.5 | 5.6 | 1.7 | 6.6 | 5.2 | 5.8 |
| Hypothetical stationary population (millions)[a] | 1,862.0 | 399.0 | 257.0 | 28.4 | 58.8 | 5.3 | 1.0 |

Source: World Bank, Social Indicators of Development 1991–2 (Johns Hopkins University Press, 1992), pp. 142, 234, 22, 286, 216, 34, 192.
a. A stationary population is one in which age- and sex-specific mortality rates have not changed over a long period and fertility rates have remained at the replacement level; that is, the net reproduction rate equals 1.

capita, among the major South Asian countries (table 2). Pakistan has shown the best long-run record of GNP growth, in the range of 5 to 6 percent over the last three decades, followed by India and Sri Lanka with growth rates close to 4 percent. Bangladesh's long-run growth rate has been only around 3 percent, while that of Nepal has been close to 3.3 percent. Within each country there have also been large fluctuations in growth from one year to the next as a result of internal factors (weather, natural calamities, civil unrest) and changes in the external environment (terms of trade, global recession, and aid flows). In the medium term policy changes have also played their part in improving or dampening economic performance.

Sectoral growth rates have varied over time and among countries. At the end of the 1980s agriculture accounted for 26 percent of GDP in Sri Lanka and Pakistan, about 30 percent in India, and nearly 40 percent in Bangladesh; industry contributed 20 to 30 percent of GDP in India, Pakistan, and Sri Lanka and only 15 percent in Bangladesh; services accounted for about 40 or 50 percent of GDP in most of the countries. The declining contribution of agriculture to GDP with no corresponding decline in its employment share has widened rural-urban income inequalities and dampened increases in real wages in agriculture. Industrial growth, besides being inadequate, has not been sufficiently labor-intensive.

### Investment and Saving

Gross domestic investment as a proportion of GDP in South Asia has risen significantly, to more than 20 percent by the end of the 1970s from levels of 10 to 15 percent three decades ago. At the end of the 1980s India, with the highest investment ratio in the region (about 23 percent), had the lowest dependence on foreign saving (about 10 percent of investment). Pakistan's investment ratio was lower (about 18 percent), but external dependence was higher (about 30 percent), while Sri Lanka and Nepal with investment ratios around 20 percent relied on foreign saving for financing 35 to 55 percent of investment. Bangladesh, with the lowest investment ratio (about 12 percent), depended most on external saving (about 80 percent of investment).

### Industry

The manufacturing sector in the South Asian countries encompasses a wide spectrum ranging from large, modern factory establishments to small-scale units, modern and traditional, and a large component of dispersed household activities such as handlooms, crafts, and artisanal occupations. In the last four

**Table 2. Output Indicators for Seven South Asian Countries, Selected Years and Periods, 1965–90**

| Indicator | India | Pakistan | Bangladesh | Sri Lanka | Nepal | Bhutan | Maldives |
|---|---|---|---|---|---|---|---|
| GNP per capita, 1990 (dollars) | 350.0 | 380.0 | 210.0 | 470.0 | 170.0 | 190.0 | 450.0 |
| Average annual growth rate of GDP (percent) | | | | | | | |
| 1965–80 | 3.6 | 5.2 | 1.7 | 4.0 | 1.9 | n.a. | n.a. |
| 1980–90 | 5.3 | 6.3 | 4.3 | 4.0 | 4.6 | 7.5 | n.a. |
| Average annual growth rate of per capita GNP, 1965–90 (percent) | 1.9 | 2.5 | 0.7 | 2.9 | 0.5 | n.a | 2.8 |
| GDP structure, 1990 (percent of total) | | | | | | | |
| Agriculture | 31.0 | 26.0 | 38.0 | 26.0 | 60.0 | 43.0 | n.a. |
| Industry | 29.0 | 25.0 | 15.0 | 26.0 | 14.0 | 27.0 | n.a. |
| Services | 40.0 | 49.0 | 46.0 | 48.0 | 26.0 | 29.0 | n.a. |

Source: World Bank, *World Development Report 1992: Development and the Environment* (Oxford University Press, 1992), pp. 218, 220, 222, 285.
n.a. Not available.

decades industrial structures have considerably broadened and diversified, particularly in India and Pakistan, extending to the chemical, fertilizer, machinery, transportation, electrical, and electronics industries. Initially, import substitution rather than exports or domestic demand was relied upon to provide the impetus for industrialization. Industry was sheltered behind high tariffs as well as quantitative import restrictions. The pessimistic policy stance toward export promotion was confirmed by high-cost, excessively protected, noncompetitive manufactures, which could not compete in world markets. Consequently, South Asia fell behind the newly industrializing countries of East Asia in exploiting exports as an engine of growth in the formative decades of the 1960s and 1970s.

Another feature of industrialization in South Asia has been extensive public sector ownership of key industries. Besides owning enterprises directly, the state has played a major role in the regulation and promotion of private enterprise in the principal South Asian countries. Industrial regulation has been pervasive, affecting the location, capacity, and technology of new units and their expansion or diversification; regulations relating to imports, foreign technology, and capital markets have also been widespread. The 1980s, however, witnessed a perceptible trend toward deregulation, export-oriented trade policy reform, some degree of privatization, and financial sector reforms in most of the region, including Pakistan, Bangladesh, Sri Lanka, Nepal, and, most recently, India.

*Infrastructure*

There has been considerable progress since decolonization in the development of infrastructure, although it continues to be overstretched and under pressure. From very low initial levels, power generation capacity by the end of the 1980s had risen to about 71,000 megawatts (MW), including some nuclear capacity in India (1,800 MW) and Pakistan (70 MW). However, commercial energy consumption levels are still low, only about two-thirds of the average for low-income economies even in India and Pakistan, which are the most advanced. In many rural areas of South Asia, especially in Nepal, energy needs are still met from fuel wood, the traditional source, at the cost of steady deforestation. In the last three decades transportation, particularly roads, has seen much improvement, and India has one of the largest railway systems in the world. However, there are wide variations between countries and between urban and rural areas within countries. There has been good progress in developing telecommunications, although numbers of telephone lines per thousand residents are still very low, especially in rural areas.

### Trade Structures

In general, external trade structures in the South Asian countries are characterized by relatively low ratios of exports to GDP, a large proportion of traditional exports in the total, and very low shares in world trade. It is encouraging that the South Asian countries have, in the last three decades, significantly reduced their dependency on importation of food and fuel. India, Pakistan, and Sri Lanka are more or less self-sufficient in foodgrains, although grain imports occur in years of shortfall and for replenishing stocks. Bangladesh, however, continues to depend on substantial food importation, most of which is financed by food aid. Nepal is an exporter of rice. Typically, crude oil and petroleum products accounted for about 15 to 20 percent of the import bill in the late 1980s; this proportion would have been much higher but for increases in the domestic production of oil, gas, and coal since the late 1970s, a development that has received considerable support from the World Bank.

### Macroeconomic Adjustment

By and large, South Asia adjusted well to the first oil shock in the early 1970s, helped by emigrant remittances and aid flows, energy import substitution, and domestic macroeconomic policies that kept inflation and fiscal deficits under reasonable control. But the decade of the 1980s, following the second oil shock, plunged the major South Asian countries into serious and continuing balance of payments problems for a variety of reasons: remittances by South Asians working abroad plateaued; aid flows registered low real increases in volume while their concessionality significantly declined as a result of changes in the composition of aid; commercial borrowings and resort to the International Monetary Fund increased, entailing heavy repayment burdens; widening fiscal deficits resulted in excessive domestic absorption spilling over into the balance of payments; large quantities of defense goods were imported (in India, Pakistan, and Sri Lanka); drought, floods (particularly in Bangladesh), civil strife (Sri Lanka), and political uncertainties toward the end of the 1980s (India, Pakistan, Bangladesh) had disruptive effects; and, most recently, the sharp although temporary impact of the 1990–91 Gulf crisis gave the economies of the region a severe jolt. These factors resulted in sizable debt accumulation in the 1980s: from a total of about $35 billion in debt outstanding and disbursed for India, Pakistan, and Bangladesh in 1980 to over $90 billion in 1989. Debt service rose by the end of the 1980s to over 20 percent of exports in India, Pakistan, and Bangladesh.

In the 1980s fiscal deficits burgeoned in India, Pakistan, and Bangladesh to around 7 to 9 percent of GDP. Sri Lanka, despite having reduced its very large fiscal imbalance around 1980, still ran a deficit of nearly 12 percent of GDP in 1989. In the context of worsening fiscal deficits and balance of payments problems, most of the South Asian countries—Pakistan, Bangladesh, Sri Lanka, Nepal, and most recently India (in 1991)—have embarked on macroeconomic stabilization and structural adjustment reforms in fiscal, trade, investment, balance of payments, and financial sector policies and in sectors such as agriculture, industry, and energy; the Bank has played a major role in stimulating and supporting these reforms.

## Human Development

Four decades ago, at the time of independence from colonial rule, all the South Asian countries with the notable exception of Sri Lanka had very low literacy rates and short life expectancies and fared poorly on other educational, health, and human development indicators. Progress since then has been steady but slow (table 3). Sri Lanka, which got an early start in human development, has achieved an adult literacy rate of 88 percent, a life expectancy of 71 years, an infant mortality rate of 19 per thousand live births, and a total fertility rate of 2.4, close to the replacement ratio. On the other hand, adult literacy is still only about 48 percent in India, 35 percent in Pakistan and Bangladesh, and 26 percent in Nepal. Life expectancies are less than 60 years in India and Pakistan and around 50 in Bangladesh, Nepal, and Bhutan. Infant mortality rates are as high as 120 per thousand in Nepal and Bhutan, and marginally below or above 100 in India, Pakistan, and Bangladesh. In each country there are wide differentials between males and females, between rural and urban populations, and across regions on principal social indicators such as literacy, female literacy, school enrollment, access to preventive and curative health facilities, and availability of safe water. Of direct concern are continuing high total fertility rates operating on large absolute population sizes alongside falling death rates. Total fertility rates are between 5 and 6 in Pakistan and Nepal and in the range of 4 to 5 in India and Bangladesh.

## Poverty and Inequality

Consistent, reliable, and comparable data on poverty and inequality are not available for the major South Asian countries.[4] The best available estimates suggest that the poverty proportion (defined as the proportion of households whose income or consumption falls below nationally stipulated poverty levels)

Table 3. **Human Development Indicators for Seven South Asian Countries**

| Indicator | India | Pakistan | Bangladesh | Sri Lanka | Nepal | Bhutan | Maldives |
|---|---|---|---|---|---|---|---|
| Life expectancy at birth (years) | 59 | 56 | 52 | 71 | 52 | 49 | 62 |
| Crude death rate (deaths per 1,000 population) | 11 | 12 | 14 | 6 | 14 | 17 | 9 |
| Infant mortality rate (infant deaths per 1,000 live births) | 92 | 103 | 105 | 19 | 121 | 123 | 70 |
| Total fertility rate[a] | 3.9 | 5.8 | 4.6 | 2.4 | 5.7 | 5.5 | 6.2 |
| Crude birth rate (births per 1,000 population) | 30 | 42 | 35 | 20 | 40 | 39 | 43 |
| Adult illiteracy (percent)[b] | | | | | | | |
| Total | 52 | 65 | 65 | 12 | 74 | 62 | n.a. |
| Female | 66 | 79 | 78 | 17 | 87 | 75 | n.a. |
| Primary school enrollment (percent of eligible population) | | | | | | | |
| Total | 98 | 38 | 70 | 107 | 86 | 26 | n.a. |
| Female | 82 | 27 | 64 | 106 | 57 | 20 | n.a. |
| Secondary school enrollment (percent of eligible population) | | | | | | | |
| Total | 43 | 20 | 17 | 74 | 30 | 5 | n.a. |
| Female | 31 | 12 | 11 | 76 | 17 | 2 | n.a. |

Source: World Bank, *Social Indicators of Development 1991–2* (Johns Hopkins University Press, 1992), pp. 142–43, 234–35, 22–23, 286–87, 216–17, 34–35, 192–93.

n.a. Not available.

a. Number of children that would be born to a woman if she were to live to the end of her childbearing years and bear children at each age in accordance with prevailing age-specific fertility rates.

b. Among persons older than 15 years of age.

in the late 1980s was as high as 70 to 80 percent in Bangladesh, about 60 percent in Nepal, 30 to 40 percent in India and Pakistan, and about 20 percent in Sri Lanka. These estimates would imply that the number of absolute poor in South Asia is on the order of 450 million, of whom about 70 percent are in India and nearly 15 percent in Bangladesh. About 80 percent of the poor are in rural areas, and in the main, urban poverty is a spillover of rural immiseration. Available evidence suggests some decline in the poverty proportion in both India and Bangladesh between the late 1970s and the mid-1980s.

The distribution of income and of land and other assets is highly skewed in all countries of the region: in India, Pakistan, and Bangladesh the income share of the poorest 20 percent of the population is typically about 8 to 9 percent, while that of the top 10 percent of the population is 25 to 30 percent. In each country the regional dimensions of poverty are important, the poorest regions being the eastern states in India, the northwest frontier and Balochistan in Pakistan, the hilly tribal areas in eastern Bangladesh, the mountainous part of Nepal, and the dry zone in northern Sri Lanka.

## Politics and Governance

India and Sri Lanka have remained vigorous, open democracies, although the Indian record was blotted by the regime's resort to emergency powers in 1975–77. Pakistan and Bangladesh have gone through prolonged periods of military or authoritarian civilian rule, but democracy was restored in the late 1980s; Nepal has moved from an absolute to a constitutional monarchy. All the South Asian countries except Nepal and Bhutan retain the bureaucratic legacy of the British colonial administration, which for all its shortcomings has provided the region with development-oriented administrative structures and capabilities. These have been sustained by a series of five-year development plans and growth in capacities for project planning and implementation.

The region has, however, been bedeviled by conflicts and tensions between and within countries. The Kashmir issue has been a major irritant in Indo-Pakistani relations, erupting into wars in 1948–49 and in 1965. The birth of Bangladesh (the former East Pakistan) as an independent state in 1971 resulted from a civil war in undivided Pakistan, followed by hostilities between India and Pakistan. Problems have arisen between landlocked Nepal and India on trade and transit, between Bangladesh and India on the use of eastern river waters, and between India and Sri Lanka over the latter's Tamil problem (Sri Lanka has been facing serious internal ethnic conflict in its north and east with its Tamil minority since 1983). Militancy has been a problem at a regional level in India and Pakistan as well. In the late 1970s Pakistan had to cope with a massive influx of refugees from Afghanistan. All this has taken its toll on current economic management, project implementation, and long-term development. Equally important, intraregional tensions have gotten in the way of closer cooperation in trade, investment, energy, irrigation and flood control, and environmental protection, in all of which there is much potential for regional coordination and cooperation.[5]

### The Development Agenda

This overview has tended to concentrate on the principal development problems of South Asia, especially as they have emerged in the last two decades. At the same time, however, the very considerable achievements of the post-colonial period should not be overlooked. Starting from very low levels of income, the countries in the region have nearly trebled their saving rates and have registered sustained growth. Much progress has been made toward food security, and famines have been prevented. Industrial structures have gained in depth and diversity. Social indicators have improved. In all this, aid has made a useful contribution.

The continuing development priorities for South Asia are also quite clear: adequate and sustained growth in per capita incomes; agricultural development to provide the basis for food security, poverty alleviation, reduction of imports and expansion of exports, and the creation of demand and supply in the large home markets; preventive and promotional measures for population control in a wider framework of human development, particularly literacy, female literacy, primary health, access to drinking water, sanitation, and nutrition; urban services oriented to the poor; domestic energy development combined with efficient and economic energy use; infrastructural development; and macroeconomic policy reforms that can contain inflation and avoid recurring fiscal and balance of payments crises. The Bank's lending operations in South Asia have been and are being addressed to this many-sided and complex agenda, and it is with reference to that agenda that the size, salience, and success of the Bank's contribution has to be assessed.

## The Bank's Lending Operations in South Asia: An Overview

South Asia includes some of the IBRD's and IDA's largest and oldest borrowers; India, Pakistan, and Sri Lanka have been borrowers since the 1950s. India, with total commitments of $35.3 billion as of the end of fiscal 1990, was in absolute terms the largest single borrower from both the IBRD and IDA. Pakistan ($7.4 billion, the seventh largest) and Bangladesh ($5.3 billion, the thirteenth largest) have also been substantial borrowers. At the end of fiscal 1990 the IBRD and IDA had cumulatively undertaken 719 lending operations in the seven South Asian countries, for a total amount of about $51 billion, of which about $23 billion or 45 percent was lent by the IBRD and about $28 billion or 55 percent by IDA (see table 4).[6]

The Bank has been an important source of external financing to the major South Asian countries (table 5), accounting for about two-fifths of all long-term debt outstanding and disbursed as of 1990 in Nepal, for about a third in India and Bangladesh, and for about a fifth in Pakistan and Sri Lanka. The Bank has a large share of official debt outstanding and disbursed in India (close to 60 percent), around 40 percent in Bangladesh and Nepal, and between 20 and 25 percent in Pakistan and Sri Lanka. India has depended almost entirely on the Bank and IDA for its multilateral borrowing, while the Asian Development Bank (ADB) and Arab multilateral funds have been important sources in the multilateral portfolios of Pakistan, Bangladesh, Sri Lanka, and Nepal.

Through fiscal 1990 South Asia received 12.5 percent of the Bank's global commitments, 50.8 percent of IDA's, and 21.4 percent of those of the Bank and IDA taken together, if lending to China is excluded, as would seem appropriate since China became a borrower only in the 1980s. South Asia's share in cumulative IDA commitments (excluding China and again through fiscal 1990), at about 51 percent, has been distinctly less than the region's share of the combined population of all low-income countries (excluding China) of 59 percent. It has also steadily declined in the last three decades: from 63.3 percent in 1961–70, to 55.3 percent in 1971–80, and to 43.2 percent in 1981–90 (table 6). This is a reflection of progressive increases in the proportion of IDA

13

**Table 4. Cumulative World Bank Lending to Seven South Asian Countries, Fiscal Year 1990**

| Country | IBRD | | IDA | | Total | |
|---|---|---|---|---|---|---|
| | Number of loans | Millions of dollars | Number of loans | Millions of dollars | Number of loans | Millions of dollars |
| India | 134 | 18,319.2 | 178 | 16,955.7 | 312 | 35,274.9 |
| Pakistan | 71 | 4,175.1 | 82 | 3,237.0 | 153 | 7,412.1 |
| Bangladesh | 1 | 46.1 | 126 | 5,248.6 | 127 | 5,294.7 |
| Sri Lanka | 12 | 210.7 | 50 | 1,323.8 | 62 | 1,534.5 |
| Nepal | ... | ... | 56 | 1,058.3 | 56 | 1,058.3 |
| Bhutan | ... | ... | 5 | 22.8 | 5 | 22.8 |
| Maldives | ... | ... | 4 | 23.9 | 4 | 23.9 |
| Total South Asia | 218 | 22,751.1 | 501 | 27,870.1 | 719 | 50,621.2 |
| *Memorandums* | | | | | | |
| All borrowers | 3,176 | 186,661.7 | 2,005 | 58,222.0 | 5,181 | 244,883.7 |
| All borrowers excluding China | 3,126 | 181,381.5 | 1,972 | 54,294.7 | 5,098 | 235,676.2 |
| South Asia's share in total (percent) | ... | 12.2 | ... | 47.9 | ... | 20.7 |
| South Asia's share in total, excluding China (percent) | ... | 12.5 | ... | 51.3 | ... | 21.5 |

Source: World Bank, "IBRD and IDA Cumulative Lending Operations, by Borrower or Guarantor, June 30, 1990," *The World Bank Annual Report 1990* (1990), pp. 178–81.

lending going to Africa in the 1970s and 1980s, and to other eligible borrowers in the 1970s (mainly Indonesia) and of the entry of China in the 1980s, claiming about a 10 percent share in IDA lending in that decade. India, IDA's largest borrower, and to a lesser extent Pakistan have had to bear the brunt of reductions over time in shares of IDA lending to South Asia.[7] It has been possible in the last decade to substantially supplement IDA credits with Bank loans to these two countries, since they have been considered creditworthy for the latter. Although this has both enabled and compensated for reductions in IDA lending to them while increasing the volume of overall lending from the Bank Group, there has been a significant loss of concessionality.

Trends from decade to decade in the nominal volume of total lending and its distribution between the Bank and IDA are shown in table 7. Total lending to South Asia in the 1970s was four times the amount lent during the 1960s, with the increase largely accounted for by IDA. Lending in the 1980s was three times that in the 1970s; this time the increase was substantially due to a step-up in IBRD lending to India and Pakistan. Reflecting these changes, IDA's proportion in total lending went up from 62 percent in 1961–70 to 84 percent in 1971–80, but dropped thereafter to 46 percent in 1981–90.

India received 70 percent of cumulative lending to South Asia up to fiscal 1990, followed by Pakistan (15 percent) and Bangladesh (10 percent). The other four countries received a combined share of 5 percent. India's share of IDA lending to South Asia (61 percent) has been significantly less than its population share in South Asia (77 percent). Pakistan's share (12 percent) has been somewhat higher than its population share (10 percent), while Bangladesh's share (19 percent) has been distinctly higher than its population share (10 percent).

MODES AND PROFILE OF LENDING. Table 8 shows that project loans have been the predominant mode of resource transfer in South Asia, accounting for 93 percent of cumulative Bank and IDA lending through fiscal 1990. Nonproject lending accounted for 6.8 percent. Specific technical assistance loans accounted for the remaining 0.2 percent and have been confined to five countries, with Bangladesh, Pakistan, and Nepal the main recipients. Within South Asia, Bangladesh has received the largest proportion of nonproject lending (28.2 percent), followed by Nepal (10.4 percent), Sri Lanka (7.1 percent), and Pakistan (5.7 percent); India's proportion is the lowest (3.8 percent).

Lending to individual countries has been subject to fluctuations and interruptions from one period to another. Apart from variations in IDA lending related to replenishment delays at various junctures, policy considerations (or

**Table 5. Long-Term Debt Outstanding and Disbursed, Five South Asian Countries, 1990**
Percent

| Source of lending | India | Pakistan | Bangladesh | Sri Lanka | Nepal | All five countries |
|---|---|---|---|---|---|---|
| *All long-term debt* | | | | | | |
| Official | 58.5 | 94.6 | 98.7 | 84.5 | 93.2 | 71.2 |
| IBRD | 12.5 | 10.3 | 0.6 | 1.7 | ... | 10.0 |
| IDA | 21.7 | 12.7 | 36.5 | 17.9 | 43.2 | 22.1 |
| Private | 41.5 | 5.4 | 1.3 | 15.5 | 6.8 | 28.8 |
| Total long-term | 100.0 | 100.0 | 100.0 | 100.0 | 100.0 | 100.0 |
| *Official debt* | | | | | | |
| Multilateral | 59.4 | 41.9 | 54.7 | 36.0 | 85.1 | 53.9 |
| IBRD | 21.4 | 10.9 | 0.6 | 2.0 | ... | 14.0 |
| IDA | 37.1 | 13.3 | 37.0 | 21.1 | 46.4 | 31.1 |
| Other | 0.9 | 17.7 | 17.1 | 12.9 | 38.7 | 8.8 |
| Bilateral | 40.6 | 58.1 | 45.3 | 64.0 | 14.9 | 46.1 |
| Total official | 100.0 | 100.0 | 100.0 | 100.0 | 100.0 | 100.0 |
| *Multilateral debt* | | | | | | |
| IBRD | 36.1 | 26.0 | 1.0 | 5.6 | ... | 26.0 |
| IDA | 62.5 | 31.9 | 67.6 | 58.7 | 54.5 | 57.7 |
| Other | 1.4 | 42.1 | 31.4 | 35.7 | 45.5 | 16.3 |
| Total multilateral | 100.0 | 100.0 | 100.0 | 100.0 | 100.0 | 100.0 |

Source: World Bank, *World Debt Tables 1990*.

"implied conditionality") have operated in determining lending levels from time to time. The 1970s witnessed a decline in the share of lending to Pakistan because of problems that persisted almost throughout that decade, such as the uncertainty consequent on Pakistan's unilateral declaration of a moratorium on repayments following the emergence of Bangladesh and, subsequently, the nationalization policies of the administration of Zulfikar Ali Bhutto (1972–77), which met with the Bank's disapproval.[8] Lending to Bangladesh in the initial years (1971–74) was confined to a few nonproject and reconstruction loans because of the Bank's insistence on Bangladesh's assuming its share of the liabilities of undivided Pakistan, and because of the country's early nationalization policies.[9] In Sri Lanka, policy differences with governments of the left-oriented Sri Lanka Freedom Party (SLFP) were reflected in reduced lending in 1961–65 and again in 1970–77.[10] In India, however, lending from the Bank and IDA taken together has followed an upward trend.

SECTORAL LENDING. Table 9 shows the sectoral distribution of project lending to South Asia in three periods: up to fiscal 1970, fiscal 1971 to fiscal 1980, and fiscal 1981–90. The 1970s witnessed large proportionate increases compared with the pre-1970 period in lending for agriculture and the social sectors, principally offset by a very steep reduction in the share of transportation. In the 1980s there was a sharp increase in lending for energy, substantially offset by a reduction in the share for agriculture. In sum, compared with the previous period, the main thrust of lending in the 1970s was for agriculture, along with continued emphasis on energy and the emergence of the social sectors as a major category. In the 1980s there was a marked shift from agriculture to energy, including a strong component of lending for the development of oil, gas, and coal.

PROJECT LENDING. The shift in the Bank's sectoral pattern of project lending in the 1970s and 1980s toward agriculture and the social sectors, which are less import-intensive than infrastructure or industrial investments, carried with it a substantial element of local procurement in goods and services earmarked for domestic bidding under loan agreements. There has also been scope for local procurement in transportation and in lending for energy, telecommunications, and industry, in which some South Asian countries, notably India with its large domestic manufacturing capacities, have been able to supply goods and services under international competitive bidding (ICB) or domestic bidding. In the late 1980s disbursements for local procurement in India were about 50 to 60 percent of total disbursements.[11] To this extent the project lending of the Bank provided "free foreign exchange" to the borrower, that is, foreign

**Table 6. Share in Total IDA Lending, and IDA Share in Total World Bank Lending, Seven South Asian Countries, by Decade, 1961–90**
Percent

| Country | Share in total IDA lending | | | | IDA lending as a share of total World Bank lending | | | |
|---|---|---|---|---|---|---|---|---|
| | 1961–70 | 1971–80 | 1981–90 | 1961–90 | 1961–70 | 1971–80 | 1981–90 | 1961–90 |
| India | 46.1 | 39.4 | 23.0 | 29.1 | 70.4 | 81.2 | 35.8 | 48.1 |
| Pakistan | 12.3 | 5.1 | 5.3 | 5.6 | 43.6 | 75.4 | 37.7 | 43.7 |
| Bangladesh | 5.5 | 7.3 | 10.1 | 9.0 | 76.6 | 100.0 | 100.0 | 99.1 |
| Sri Lanka | 0.9 | 1.9 | 2.5 | 2.3 | 26.2 | 100.0 | 89.1 | 86.3 |
| Nepal | 0.1 | 1.3 | 2.2 | 1.8 | 100.0 | 100.0 | 100.0 | 100.0 |
| Bhutan | 0.0 | 0.0 | 0.1 | 0.04 | 0.0 | 0.0 | 100.0 | 100.0 |
| Maldives | 0.0 | 0.02 | 0.1 | 0.04 | 0.0 | 100.0 | 100.0 | 100.0 |
| Total South Asia | 64.9 | 55.0 | 43.2 | 47.9 | 62.2 | 83.6 | 46.2 | 55.9 |

Source: Author's calculations based on World Bank data.

**Table 7. IBRD and IDA Lending to South Asia, by Decade, 1960–69**
Millions of U.S. Dollars

| Period | IBRD | IDA | Total | IDA share in total (percent) |
|---|---|---|---|---|
| Through 1960 | 787.9 | 0.0 | 787.9 | 0.0 |
| 1961–70 | 1,086.7 | 1,786.6 | 2,873.3 | 62.2 |
| 1971–80 | 1,920.0 | 9,806.2 | 11,726.2 | 83.6 |
| 1981–90 | 18,956.5 | 16,277.3 | 35,233.8 | 46.2 |
| Through 1990 | 22,751.1 | 27,870.1 | 50,621.2 | 55.1 |

Source: Author's calculations based on World Bank data.

exchange usable for the indirect external costs of Bank projects, for project and nonproject imports other than those financed by the Bank (developmental or otherwise) or debt servicing, or for augmenting reserves. Also, the counterpart funds arising from such foreign exchange provided budget support.

The loosening of the format of project lending in the last two decades has also tended to blur the distinction between project and program lending. In the major South Asian countries there has been substantial intermediation through development financing institutions (DFIs), agricultural credit institutions, and other intermediaries. Financing of outlays in specific periods of time in an ongoing project or program (time-slice financing) has been undertaken in the railways, telecommunications, and irrigation for medium-term projects and programs of sectors, entities, or states (in India). Sector loans have permitted the use of funds for a variety of projects and activities in agriculture, industry, and transport. Similarly, industrial restructuring loans have permitted capital investment, modernization, and rehabilitation covering multiple units in various industries. Some loans, especially in irrigation and transportation, have been in the nature of lines of credit available for numerous small-scale individual projects such as tubewells, minor irrigation schemes, tanks, rural roads, and so on. Notably in India, single-project loans have covered investments and activities in a number of states and localities.

The average loan in South Asia has been about 50 percent larger than the average for all borrowers from the Bank Group. In nominal terms, for the region as a whole, the average project loan increased from $22 million in the pre-1970 period to $47 million in 1971–80 and $109 million in 1981–90. Apart from inflation, several factors contributed to this trend. Large investments in

**Table 8. Cumulative World Bank Lending to South Asia, by Country and Type of Loan, as of Fiscal Year 1990**
Millions of U.S. Dollars

| Country or region | Project lending | Nonproject lending | Technical assistance | Total |
|---|---|---|---|---|
| India | 33,944.9 (96.2) | 1,330.0 (3.8) | 0.0 (0.0) | 35,274.9 |
| Pakistan | 6,971.1 (94.0) | 420.0 (5.7) | 21.0 (0.3) | 7,412.1 |
| Bangladesh | 3,737.7 (70.6) | 1,492.5 (28.2) | 64.5 (1.2) | 5,294.7 |
| Sri Lanka | 1,422.1 (92.7) | 109.4 (7.1) | 3.0 (0.2) | 1,534.5 |
| Nepal | 939.3 (88.7) | 110.0 (10.4) | 9.0 (0.9) | 1,058.3 |
| Bhutan | 19.8 (86.8) | 0.0 (0.0) | 3.0 (13.2) | 22.8 |
| Maldives | 23.9 (100.0) | 0.0 (0.0) | 0.0 (0.0) | 23.9 |
| Total South Asia | 47,058.8 (93.0) | 3,461.9 (6.8) | 100.5 (0.2) | 50,621.2 |
| Asia (other than South Asia) | 46,264.4 (92.6) | 3,600.9 (7.2) | 100.7 (0.2) | 49,966.0 |
| Africa | 30,203.7 (85.7) | 4,238.5 (12.0) | 809.7 (2.3) | 35,251.9 |
| LAC[a] | 57,476.3 (91.5) | 5,080.7 (8.1) | 256.5 (0.4) | 62,813.5 |
| EMENA (excluding Pakistan)[a] | 41,398.8 (89.5) | 4,750.9 (10.3) | 81.4 (0.2) | 46,231.1 |
| Total | 222,402.0 (90.8) | 21,132.9 (8.6) | 1,348.8 (0.6) | 244,883.7 |

Source: Author's calculations based on World Bank data. Figures in parentheses are percentages of country or regional totals.
a. LAC = Latin America and the Caribbean; EMENA = Europe, Middle East, and North Africa.

infrastructure, industry, and irrigation were both necessary and possible because of the geographic and economic size of the principal South Asian countries, notably India. Lending through financial intermediation and by multistate and multicomponent loans in recent years has increased loan sizes, especially of loans for agricultural credit and irrigation, which have been of a substantial order. Growth in the proportion of lending for energy in the 1970s and 1980s was another major factor. Large, loosely structured, and complex projects in recent years have had an impact on staff requirements for project preparation, appraisal, and supervision, and on project performance. They have also added to the problems of monitoring and evaluation.

AID COORDINATION. The Bank has played an important role in South Asia in mobilizing and coordinating aid through consortiums and consultative groups under its chairmanship. The earliest consortium was for India in 1958, followed by the Pakistan consortium in 1960. The Sri Lanka aid group came into being in 1965. After some initial hesitancy on the part of Bangladesh, a consultative group was set up for that country in 1973. There is also an aid group for Nepal. Participants in Bank-sponsored consortia and consultative groups include, apart from the Bank and IDA, Development Assistance Committee member bilateral donors and the ADB, Arab funds, European Economic Community, and the International Fund for Agricultural Development among multilateral donors. The Bank has also catalyzed aid from other sources. In 1975–87 about a third of Bank projects in South Asia attracted cofinancing, mainly from official bilateral sources, amounting in those projects to about two-fifths of total lending from external sources.

IMPLEMENTATION EXPERIENCE. The Bank's performance indicators relating to project implementation in the South Asian countries have been somewhat above the average for all borrowers from the Bank and IDA during most of the last two decades.[12] Basically, three types of factors have affected project performance in South Asia. The first are force majeure disruptions such as those caused by wars, civil strife, and natural calamities, which have affected a number of South Asian countries during various periods in the last two decades. The second are factors specific to projects; the Bank classifies these as managerial, technical, financial, and political.[13] Political and financial commitments to Bank projects have been relatively satisfactory in South Asia. Technical problems have varied from project to project, depending in part on the adequacy and quality of project preparation and appraisal. Managerial efficiency in project implementation has, however, been a matter of serious concern in most countries. The third set of factors comprises countrywide

**Table 9. Project Lending in South Asia, by Sector and Decade, Fiscal Years 1970–90**

| Sector | Up to FY 1970 | | | FY 1971–FY 1980 | | | FY 1981–FY 1990 | | | Up to FY 1990 | | |
|---|---|---|---|---|---|---|---|---|---|---|---|---|
| | Number of loans | Millions of dollars | Percent of total | Number of loans | Millions of dollars | Percent of total | Number of loans | Millions of dollars | Percent of total | Number of loans | Millions of dollars | Percent of total |
| Infrastructure | 69 | 1,706.3 | 56.8 | 46 | 3,508.0 | 34.6 | 89 | 15,741.6 | 46.4 | 204 | 20,955.9 | 44.5 |
| Energy | 22 | 455.4 | 14.8 | 21 | 2,249.3 | 22.2 | 60 | 11,955.1 | 35.3 | 103 | 14,649.8 | 31.1 |
| Oil, gas, and coal | 3 | 73.7 | 2.4 | 3 | 240.0 | 2.4 | 17 | 2,958.0 | 8.7 | 23 | 3,271.7 | 6.9 |
| Power | 19 | 371.7 | 12.4 | 18 | 2,009.3 | 19.8 | 43 | 8,997.1 | 26.5 | 80 | 11,378.1 | 24.2 |
| Transportation | 41 | 1,098.2 | 36.6 | 16 | 794.7 | 7.8 | 23 | 2,930.5 | 8.6 | 80 | 4,823.4 | 10.3 |
| Telecommunications | 6 | 162.7 | 5.4 | 9 | 464.0 | 4.6 | 6 | 856.0 | 2.5 | 21 | 1,482.7 | 3.1 |
| Industry | 28 | 655.9 | 21.8 | 33 | 1,637.7 | 16.1 | 47 | 5,056.0 | 14.9 | 108 | 7,349.6 | 15.6 |
| Agriculture and rural development | 31 | 556.2 | 18.5 | 109 | 3,923.9 | 38.7 | 119 | 8,936.5 | 26.4 | 259 | 13,416.6 | 28.5 |
| Social sectors | 7 | 85.8 | 2.9 | 30 | 1,077.5 | 10.6 | 57 | 4,166.8 | 12.3 | 94 | 5,330.1 | 11.4 |
| Total project lending | 135 | 3,004.2 | 100.0 | 218 | 10,153.7[a] | 100.0 | 312 | 33,900.9 | 100.0 | 665 | 47,058.8[a] | 100.0 |
| *Memorandums* | | | | | | | | | | | | |
| Nonproject lending | 8 | 655.0 | ... | 20 | 1,545.0 | ... | 13 | 1,261.9 | ... | 41 | 3,461.9 | ... |
| Technical assistance | 1 | 2.0 | ... | 5 | 27.5 | ... | 7 | 71.0 | ... | 13 | 100.5 | ... |
| Total lending | 144 | 3,661.2 | ... | 243 | 11,726.2 | ... | 332 | 35,233.8 | ... | 719 | 50,621.2 | ... |

Source: Author's calculations based on World Bank data.
a. Includes $6.6 million in supplementary commitments to a number of reactivated projects in Bangladesh.

macroeconomic, sectoral, and intersectoral problems (for example, inflation, balance of payments constraints, and shortages of commodities and infrastructural inputs), which affect projects but over which project executing agencies may have little or no control. Such factors have affected all projects, whether financed by the Bank or by other sources.

Repayment covenants have been honored in South Asia without default, even in times of grave balance of payments difficulties, except for a brief interregnum in Pakistan pending the assumption of liabilities by Bangladesh upon its independence. In a number of cases other covenants, such as those relating to audit, staffing, and institutional matters, have not been fulfilled adequately or on schedule. But in the main these have not jeopardized implementation. There have been delays and difficulties in the funding of domestic resources, particularly in projects executed by the state and provincial governments of India and Pakistan, respectively. Budgetary resources at these levels are more constrained and under greater pressure than at the central level. Furthermore, whereas the central government has a direct incentive in speeding the utilization of aid to augment foreign exchange availability, states and provinces are primarily concerned with their domestic budgetary problems.

Part of the domestic funding problem in the 1980s relates to currency depreciation, which has entailed increases in project scope and required increased local currency funding for absorbing loan amounts in full. Procedural delays in enlarging projects and nonavailability of domestic funds in the short run have both contributed to lags in utilization. Covenants on which compliance has been least satisfactory in South Asia, as elsewhere, are those whereby the Bank has sought to influence sectorwide or economywide reforms through its lending for individual projects or for groups of repeat projects. Such cases have mostly related to revenue covenants and to the imposition or revision of rates and tariffs in energy, transport, irrigation, and urban water supply projects. Covenants relating to prompt loan recoveries and recoveries of receivables by financial and other intermediaries have also encountered difficulties in compliance.

Enforcement of procurement procedures is an important aspect of project lending operations. While South Asian borrowers are by now quite familiar with the Bank's procurement and bidding procedures, difficulties have arisen in many projects for a variety of administrative reasons, such as delays in finalizing bid specifications, evaluation of offers, and placing of contracts. Disputes have also arisen at a substantive level, particularly in India, about the scope for domestic bidding, short-listing of foreign sources, and choice of technology.

Many of these problems have their roots in India's strong desire to maximize the utilization of domestic manufacturing capabilities. In a number of sectors and subsectors (for example, power, railways, telecommunications, agricultural credit, and fertilizer projects) procurement issues in India have led to substantial implementation delays as well. However, the Bank's strict enforcement of fair and open procurement procedures has gone a long way toward preventing corruption, arbitrariness, and malpractice in the placement and enforcement of contracts, in which the countries of South Asia, as others elsewhere, have not been otherwise blemishless. One can, however, never be sure that there has been no corruption at all at any level or in any form in Bank projects. Kickbacks, for instance, can be sought and received even from a properly chosen supplier, and malpractice at the stage of execution is a possibility.

Disbursement ratios (the proportion of disbursements to cumulative commitments at the beginning of the year) are a summary indicator of progress in project implementation. The slowdown of disbursement ratios and the buildup of project pipelines were matters of concern in the late 1980s, especially in India and Bangladesh. In India, undisbursed balances at the end of the 1980s in Bank loans and IDA credits amounted to nearly $12 billion, equivalent to about four years of current commitment levels. Overall project aid in the pipeline in Bangladesh rose from about $2 billion in 1981 to about $5 billion at the end of the decade, while disbursement ratios steeply declined, from 28 percent to 19 percent. Performance in individual projects aside, the capacity of the system as a whole to absorb project lending is showing clear signs of stress in these countries. The sectoral and structural adjustment lending operations of the Bank in the major South Asian countries in the 1980s and early 1990s are a response to this phase in South Asia, in which, in the words of one of the Bank's annual reviews (ARIS, 1982), "the interaction between project lending and other lending instruments available to the Bank (sector and program lending, SALs) becomes particularly important if further progress is to be achieved."

## The Lending Experience in South Asia: 1971–90

With the preceding sections as background, we proceed to examine the Bank's project lending experience in the 1970s and 1980s at the sectoral level and with special reference to major South Asian borrowers.[14] The 1970s and 1980s account for 80 percent by number and 94 percent by value of all project lending by the Bank up to 1990 in South Asia. The four major borrowers we have concentrated on—India, Pakistan, Bangladesh, and Sri Lanka—account for 89 percent of numbers of projects and 98 percent of lending money in the 1971–90 period. Table 10, which gives a breakdown of project lending operations for the four countries during this period by major sector, provides the framework in terms of dimensions and relative priorities for the discussion of individual sectors that follows.

### Energy

Energy has been the leading sector for Bank activity, claiming nearly a third ($14.6 billion) of the Bank's cumulative project lending. The share of lending to the sector increased significantly, from about 15 percent of project lending before 1970 to about 22 percent in the 1970s and 35 percent in the 1980s. Table 11 shows the pattern of lending in the energy sector in the 1971–90 period. Resource endowments in South Asia for energy development have made possible the growth and diversification of the Bank's project lending in this sector. Sharply increased lending for oil, natural gas, and coal in the 1970s and 1980s has greatly aided balance of payments adjustment. The Bank's long familiarity with the sector, its ability to extend large loans that are open to worldwide procurement, its flexible approach in lending to different types of investments, and its analytical work in the area of sector studies have all been of great value to borrowers. Bank loans have also utilized domestic capacities (for generation equipment in India, for example, and for pipeline construction in India and Pakistan).

INDIA. In India, transmission and distribution (T&D), including rural electrification, was the main emphasis in power sector lending in the 1970s and

Table 10. Project Lending for Four Countries in South Asia, by Sector, Fiscal Years 1971–90

| Sector | India Number of loans | India Millions of dollars | Pakistan Number of loans | Pakistan Millions of dollars | Bangladesh Number of loans | Bangladesh Millions of dollars | Sri Lanka Number of loans | Sri Lanka Millions of dollars |
|---|---|---|---|---|---|---|---|---|
| Energy | 42 | 11,488.5 (35.2) | 17 | 1,654.5 (27.1) | 11 | 882.3 (25.0) | 6 | 196.7 (15.1) |
| Transportation | 13 | 2,463.3 (7.7) | 17 | 530.0 (8.7) | 9 | 437.6 (12.4) | 4 | 171.5 (13.1) |
| Telecommunications | 6 | 1,017.0 (3.2) | 3 | 176.0 (2.9) | 2 | 55.0 (1.6) | 1 | 30.0 (2.3) |
| Industry | 31 | 4,663.8 (14.5) | 20 | 1,216.5 (20.0) | 15 | 604.9 (17.1) | 8 | 167.3 (12.8) |
| Agriculture and rural development | 111 | 9,202.2 (28.6) | 35 | 1,745.2 (28.6) | 33 | 941.6 (26.6) | 22 | 554.6 (42.5) |
| Education | 3 | 552.0 (1.7) | 7 | 400.2 (6.6) | 8 | 370.1 (10.5) | 2 | 77.5 (5.9) |
| Population, health, and nutrition | 9 | 594.3 (1.8) | 1 | 18.0 (0.3) | 3 | 125.0 (3.5) | 1 | 17.5 (1.3) |
| Urbanization | 14 | 1,365.3 (4.2) | 3 | 176.0 (2.9) | 1 | 47.6 (1.3) | 2 | 13.0 (1.0) |
| Water supply and sewerage | 12 | 986.9 (3.1) | 3 | 176.6 (2.9) | 3 | 72.0 (2.0) | 3 | 76.2 (6.0) |
| Total | 241 | 32,133.3 (100.0) | 96 | 6,093.0 (100.0) | 85 | 3,542.7[a] (100.0) | 49 | 1,304.3 (100.0) |

Source: Author's calculations based on World Bank data. Figures in parentheses are percentages of column totals.
a. Includes $6.6 million for a number of reactivated projects.

**Table 11. World Bank Energy Lending for Four South Asian Countries, Fiscal Years 1971–90**
Millions of U.S. dollars

| Subsector | India | Pakistan | Bangladesh | Sri Lanka |
|---|---|---|---|---|
| Electric power | 8,594.2 | 1,378.0 | 664.3 | 196.7 |
| Generation | 6,412.0 | 183.0 | 92.0 | 42.7 |
| Thermal | 4,134.2 | 183.0 | 92.0 | 42.7 |
| Hydroelectric | 2,277.8 | 0.0 | 0.0 | 0.0 |
| Transmission and distribution | 1,295.7 | 457.0 | 211.0 | 154.0 |
| Rural electrification | 536.5 | 160.0 | 184.0 | 0.0 |
| Sectoral and multipurpose | 350.0 | 578.0 | 177.3 | 0.0 |
| Technical assistance | 0.0 | 0.0 | 0.0 | 0.0 |
| Oil, gas, and coal | 2,694.3 | 276.5 | 218.0 | 0.0 |
| Oil and gas exploration and development | 1,615.3 | 166.5 | 218.0 | 0.0 |
| Pipelines | 340.0 | 103.0 | 0.0 | 0.0 |
| Coal exploration and development | 739.0 | 7.0 | 0.0 | 0.0 |
| Total | 11,288.5 | 1,654.5 | 882.3 | 196.7 |

Source: World Bank, *Annual Report,* various years.

early 1980s. Many of the loans catered to individual states in different regions of India and provided for strengthening of regional grids for energy transfers. Starting in the late 1970s, the Bank turned to financing large generation and allied transmission facilities through superthermal stations (units of 500 MW capacity or greater) close to sources of coal and built by the National Thermal Power Corporation (NTPC), a central-government entity set up for the purpose. This shift was influenced in part by increased domestic capability in India to produce generating equipment and in part by the Bank's preference for centralized generation on grounds of economy and efficiency. In this period, apart from a few loans routed through central-level intermediaries such as the Rural Electrification Corporation and the Power Finance Corporation, the Bank's exposure to state electricity boards (SEBs) was limited, although it was shifting toward them in the later 1980s; so far there have been no sectoral adjustment loans.

Since the Bank overcame its ideological inhibition against lending for oil and gas development, it has kept up a steady stream of project financing in this area. This has been a significant contribution to technology transfer from sources other than the Soviet Union, on which India's Oil and Natural Gas Commission had been entirely dependent, and to reducing dependence on oil imports. One of the early loans of the Bank was to private sector coal mines in India, but following the nationalization of the coal mines in 1973, the Bank opted out of coal development until 1984 when it made a loan to Coal India, the public sector entity in this field, to be followed by further lending in subsequent years.

PAKISTAN. Three distinct phases are apparent in the history of Bank lending for the energy sector in Pakistan. During the 1960s the Bank was heavily involved in hydroelectric projects arising from the Indus Waters treaty, the hydropower stations at Mangla and Tarbela being the major investments. The first loan to Pakistan's Water and Power Development Authority (WAPDA) was made in 1970, but during 1972–74 a hiatus in lending for the energy sector followed, a consequence of the slowing down of the Bank's overall lending to Pakistan in the 1970s. Between the mid-1970s and the mid-1980s there were a series of loans for T&D. In the second half of the 1980s there were a couple of loans each for generation and for T&D, including one for rural electrification. This period also saw two loans for energy sector adjustment and one for stimulating private investment in energy development. One of the earliest loans to Pakistan (1954) was for the pipeline from the Sui gas field; four more loans followed for extending the pipeline to provide feedstock for fertilizer and power plants. Other loans have supported exploration assistance to the public sector Oil and Gas Development Corporation, the development of the Toot oil field, refinery improvements, and a geological survey for prospecting for coal in Balochistan. In both power and natural gas the Bank's emphasis on T&D and on pipelines has appropriately reflected the fact that hydroplants and gas fields are distant from demand centers in Pakistan.[15]

BANGLADESH. With limited hydroelectric potential and little access to coal, Bangladesh is heavily dependent on natural gas, of which the country's eastern region has substantial reserves. The rural areas are very poorly served by electricity. Against this background, Bank lending has heavily concentrated on natural gas development, oil and gas exploration, T&D in the power sector, and a couple of loans for rural electrification through cooperatives. In 1989

Bangladesh received a sectoral adjustment loan to support resource development, institutional reforms and investment, and pricing and demand management.

SRI LANKA. The Bank's involvement in Sri Lanka's energy sector has suffered from the vicissitudes of its overall relationship with that country. In the pre-1970 period, loans for the power sector (1954, 1959, 1961, and thereafter only in 1969 and 1970) were made mostly when governments of the United National Party were in power. For almost a decade thereafter, between 1970 and 1979, there was only one small transmission loan in the Colombo area. Essentially, toward the end of the 1970s the Bank had lost contact with the power sector in Sri Lanka, leaving it to bilateral donors to finance the large hydroelectric projects of the Mahaweli development program. However, an effort to get back on track was initiated in 1982 in an energy sector assessment study conducted jointly by the Bank and the United Nations Development Programme (UNDP). Later loans, except for a diesel generating station in 1982, have been for T&D, including a time-slice loan in 1988 for the Electricity Board's five-year distribution program.

IMPLEMENTATION. Implementation in energy sector projects appears to have been generally satisfactory. Serious delays have occurred in only a few projects, and strong competition among suppliers in the 1980s has contained import costs. Available project performance audit reports (PPARs) indicate that shortcomings in project preparation have affected performance in some projects. Among the shortcomings have been optimistic demand forecasts (for the Sri Lanka IV power project and the Bakhrabad gas project in Bangladesh), insufficient risk analysis (the Second Toot oil field in Pakistan), and inadequate field investigations (the Kulekhani hydroelectric project in Nepal). Land acquisition delays have also been a factor. NTPC's Singrauli thermal project and the Bombay High oil and gas project in India, and the energy sector adjustment loan to Pakistan, are examples of successful implementation, although Singrauli has given rise to serious environmental problems.

PROBLEMS OF THE POWER SECTOR. The basic problem in the power sector in South Asia, as among other Bank borrowers, is that large investments and generally satisfactory physical execution of individual projects have not been accompanied by better system performance.[16] Investment planning has been oriented to increasing supply, to the relative neglect of efficiency and economy in operations, demand management, and energy conservation. T&D has lagged behind investments in generation. Quality of service in many utilities is poor, leading to damage or unusability of equipment and to reliance on high-cost captive facilities among users.

Total network losses, technical and nontechnical (the latter include losses due to theft and inadequate billing and collection) have been very high in many South Asian countries, ranging from around 20 percent in India and Sri Lanka to between 25 and 40 percent in Pakistan and Bangladesh. The sustainability of projects is gravely threatened by poor financial performance, reflected in inadequate internal resource generation, low or negative returns on investment, and high levels of commercial receivables. Average tariffs have consistently trailed behind costs, and industrial consumers cross-subsidize underpriced electricity for agricultural and residential users.[17] Increasingly, environmental problems have also emerged, mainly in the form of emissions and fly ash accumulation in thermal plants and siltation of hydroelectric reservoirs.

THE POLICY DIALOGUE. In its long association with the power sector in India, the Bank has been involved in a continual dialogue on financial matters. In the 1970s the Bank was able to persuade the government to appoint a high-level committee to prescribe financial norms to SEBs.[18] Subsequently, in 1985, a statutory requirement was placed on them to achieve a minimum rate of return of 3 percent on assets after providing fully for depreciation and interest. In practice, most SEBs have not been able to meet the norm, largely because of subsidized power to agriculture.

Although the Bank has had a long-term direct stake in reducing agricultural power subsidies, arising from its lending both for rural electrification and for irrigation pumpsets, its leverage for upgrading financial performance has been ineffective for a number of reasons. To begin with, the Bank's direct lending to individual SEBs and its continuous involvement with any one of them have been limited; financial covenants, to the extent imposed, have been inadequately fulfilled or postponed. Faced with this situation, the Bank increasingly turned in the 1980s to financing investments in central-government-owned operations—mainly the large generating plants of the NTPC—hoping thereby to exercise policy influence directly at the central-government level and indirectly through the NTPC over state-level utilities. Although the Bank has been able to make a significant contribution to institution building in the NTPC itself, its expectation of using the NTPC to secure reforms in the SEBs has not been realized. Instead, the continued poor financial situation of the SEBs has been transmitted to the NTPC in the form of large arrearages for power purchases, reflected as unsupportable levels of receivables in the NTPC's accounts.

This development once again turned the Bank toward the SEBs in the later 1980s. The greatest handicap in promoting managerial and financial reforms in the SEBs arises from the fact that, under the Indian Constitution, power sector development is a responsibility assigned to the states. The central government has little leverage over the states, since the bulk of its developmental assistance to them is entitlement-based and not linked to performance conditionalities. In these circumstances the Bank's options are limited: it could either reduce or suspend lending until needed reforms are implemented; or it could continue to intermediate through central entities on condition that they, in turn, exercise effective leverage over the states; or it could try to exert leverage over the SEBs directly. At the close of the 1980s the Bank was trying all three options.

The question remains whether the Bank should have tried to exercise more effective leverage earlier instead of allowing problems to accumulate to the extent they have in India's power system. As a practical matter, the Bank's only recourse would have been to withdraw from lending in an attempt to enforce financial and other covenants, but such a course, considering the size of the loans in the energy sector, would have considerably slowed achievement of its lending targets besides disrupting additions to capacity in this crucially important sector. On the other hand, given the very large investment requirements for energy development in prospect, the Bank's contribution in the future is likely to be proportionately less than in the past, and therefore so is its ability to promote reform. It could be argued then that, because of the "unquestioned funding of power needs," the Bank has acquiesced in postponing reforms to a point where they have become urgent and complicated on the one hand, while on the other the Bank's possible influence in seeing that they are effectively tackled has become diluted. There can be no easy resolution of this dilemma, especially in retrospect.

In the other major South Asian countries, which have been free from India's center-state problems, the Bank's institutional interaction has been confined to central electricity authorities. Such interaction has not been without problems, but they have been of a different kind from those posed in India. Paradoxically, whereas the pressure for continued lending at a rapid pace has inhibited the policy dialogue in India, discontinuities in lending have had the same result in Pakistan and Sri Lanka. The hiatus during the early 1970s in lending for power in Pakistan reduced the Bank's capacity to influence reforms in energy pricing and improvements in WAPDA's functioning; the Bank had to wait until the sectoral adjustment loans of the mid-1980s to acquire more comprehensive leverage. In Sri Lanka the Bank pressed for the establishment of the Ceylon Electricity Board (CEB) as early as 1958, but by the time the CEB finally came into being in 1969, the Bank had entered into its long period of hibernation, which was to last until the end of the 1970s. There was thus an effective loss of policy dialogue in Sri Lanka for nearly two decades in this sector. In Bangladesh management and financial problems in utility functioning, although noted in Bank documents throughout the 1980s, began to be comprehensively addressed only in the sectoral adjustment loan of 1989.

In South Asia current low levels of commercial energy consumption, steady demand growth at around 10 percent per year (two to three times the rate of GDP growth), and escalating unit costs of investment add up to large requirements for additional capacity and for financial resources to make them possible.[19] If the Bank is to continue to play an important role in the energy sector, it will have to complement its own lendable resources with significant cofinancing from official and private sources and use its lending to promote major reforms in the operational and financial functioning of its borrower agencies. This will require an optimal combination of project and sectoral lending instruments, effective institutional interaction at various levels, and dogged policy dialogue. The Bank has entered into this phase in Pakistan, Bangladesh, and Sri Lanka and is poised to do so in India. In Pakistan and Bangladesh sectoral adjustment loans are addressed to better planning, reduction of subsidies in power and natural gas pricing, energy conservation, rehabilitation and modernization of equipment, and improvements to system operation and maintenance. In India and Sri Lanka the detailed sector studies that the Bank has undertaken provide the basis for policy options to the borrowers and for charting the Bank's own lending modalities and priorities in the years ahead.

### Transportation

Transportation was by far the leading sector in South Asia in the Bank's pre-1970 project lending portfolio, claiming a share of about 37 percent. The proportion sharply declined to 8 to 9 percent in the 1970s and 1980s. Table 12 provides an analysis by subsector of transportation lending in 1971–90.

RAILWAYS. The Bank has had a long-term relationship with the Indian Railways (IR) since 1949 and made sixteen loans totaling about $1.5 billion up to the end of the 1980s to this single entity. The first thirteen loans were essentially time-slice program loans for locomotives, rolling stock, line capacity, track renewal, electrification, and system additions based on successive medium-term plans of the railways. In contrast, from the fourteenth loan (1987–88) onward special attention was paid to corporate planning, technological upgrading through specific project components (such as funding for a new wheel and axle plant), production facilities for diesel and electric locomotives, workshop

**Table 12. World Bank Transportation Lending for Four South Asian Countries, Fiscal Years 1971–90**
Millions of U.S. dollars

| Subsector | India | Pakistan | Bangladesh | Sri Lanka |
|---|---|---|---|---|
| Railways | 1,525.7 | 110.0 | 0.0 | 0.0 |
| Roads | 604.6 | 202.0 | 338.9 | 118.5 |
| Highways | 450.0 | 202.0 | 118.0 | 40.5 |
| Rural roads | 154.6 | 0.0 | 62.3 | 0.0 |
| Rehabilitation | 0.0 | 0.0 | 158.6 | 78.0 |
| Sector loan | 0.0 | 184.0 | 0.0 | 0.0 |
| Ports | 250.0 | 34.0 | 85.0 | 0.0 |
| Tankers | 83.0 | 0.0 | 0.0 | 0.0 |
| Inland water transport | 0.0 | 0.0 | 13.7 | 0.0 |
| Bus transport | 0.0 | 0.0 | 0.0 | 53.0 |
| Total | 2,463.3 | 530.0 | 437.6 | 107.0 |

Source: World Bank, *Annual Report,* various years.

modernization and rationalization, and centralized unit exchange facilities for locomotive maintenance.

In general, loans to the IR have been successfully implemented, although delays have occurred in some cases because freight demand has been below projections. In the second-generation loans the main problem area has been the establishment of modern centralized maintenance facilities for locomotives. The IR has resisted this component, largely because of the significant staff redundancy it would have entailed. As a result the Bank's evaluators came to recognize that in the IR any component that is likely to have a substantial impact on the level or deployment of labor is going to experience serious difficulties.[20] As regards financial performance, the IR has been able to meet its statutory dividend requirement of about 5 percent on capital to the government, taking one year with another, but depreciation provisions have been underfunded—a matter of concern in the context of heavy replacement requirements for aging track and rolling stock. Freight traffic subsidizes passenger traffic, in which demand growth and public pressure are strong; subsidies to commuter traffic and losses on uneconomic lines are large. Overstaffing is significant in the IR's labor force of nearly 2 million. The Bank has been well aware of these problems, but its policy dialogue on these issues has not been particularly sustained or successful despite its long association with the IR.

Railway loans to Pakistan have been much smaller, aggregating to $110 million spread over eleven loans. Implementation was not satisfactory in some of the earlier loans; operational and financial problems have been of the same kind as in India, only perhaps worse. A review carried out after the eleventh railway project in Pakistan noted that "the borrower did little or nothing of what the Bank asked, and yet rather than ask why, the Bank simply repeated the same conditionality, adding more specifics and more targets."[21]

ROADS. Three broad types of investments have been financed in the roads subsector: important national highways (including bridges) or segments thereof in all major South Asian countries; rural roads in India and Bangladesh; and rehabilitation of roads damaged in floods in Bangladesh and damaged as a result of ethnic conflict in the late 1980s in Sri Lanka. In addition, a sectoral loan combining rail and road inputs has been made to Pakistan ($184 million). The Bank's thrust in this subsector has been to introduce modern standards of design, construction, and maintenance; to encourage institution building at the governmental level by supporting the creation and strengthening of highway departments (especially in Pakistan, Bangladesh, and Sri Lanka); and to strengthen the local construction industry by providing equipment and training (Pakistan, Bangladesh, and Sri Lanka).

A number of road projects have encountered serious delays and cost overruns, especially in Pakistan and Bangladesh. The main problems have been delays in land acquisition, fragmentation of contracts, technical and financial inadequacies of the local construction industry, and poor coordination on the part of executing agencies. Yet economic rates of return have been high, in part explained by rising fuel costs in the last two decades. Although a number of agricultural and irrigation projects have included components for rural roads, specific lending for this purpose, despite its importance, has been limited: only 15 percent of lending for roads in 1971–90 and mainly confined to Bangladesh and to two states in India. The reason is that the Bank has been reluctant to face problems in design, appraisal, intermediation, and supervision inherent in financing large numbers of dispersed individual works.

As part of its lending to the transport sector, the Bank has been instrumental in promoting transport coordination studies in India and Pakistan. The studies have produced useful recommendations relating to intermodal coordination of traffic, especially with a view to fuel conservation, but their impact on policy has been limited, and no serious dialogue to follow up on these studies has taken place.

Transportation lending had to accept a sharp downturn in its share in Bank lending in the 1970s and 1980s. The broad issue that arises in this context is whether the Bank's interventions could have been more sharply focused in terms of subsectoral priorities, possible alternative types of projects within them, and policy dialogue. Prima facie, it would seem that the Bank's concentration on and well-established relationship with the Indian Railways has blunted the Bank's influence on wider policy matters: transport policy and coordination, financial performance of railways and ports, and maintenance standards for roads. This is not, however, due entirely to the Bank's passivity but is also to be explained by political problems (for example, overmanning and social burdens at the IR) and the diffuseness, in space and over time, of the lending pattern in this sector.

## Industry

Apart from project lending, the Bank Group's support to industry includes IFC's operations and program lending to sustain and increase industrial output. Project lending to industry itself has been highly diversified, and this diversity is not adequately captured in the Bank's threefold classification of lending for this sector into industry, development financing institutions (DFIs), and small-scale enterprises (SSEs). Table 13 presents a more specific analysis of industrial lending during 1971–90 by country. The bulk of it has been for fertilizer and petrochemical projects (41 percent) and for on-lending through DFIs (48 percent).

FERTILIZERS AND PETROCHEMICALS. The Bank's rationale and motivation for financing fertilizer production in South Asia stem from several factors. Fertilizer use has become a sine qua non for increasing agricultural output with the introduction in the mid-1960s of new technology based on high-yielding seeds. Consumption of chemical fertilizers has been rapidly increasing in the major South Asian countries, which are also endowed with domestic feedstock resources to support local manufacture. Given the demand, supply, and price fluctuations in world fertilizer markets, in which their own needs are a large factor, it makes sense for the major South Asian countries to create a domestic manufacturing base in order to create cost-effective substitutes for imports and reduce their exposure to the vagaries of the world market.

Until the late 1960s the Bank was unwilling to lend for public sector enter-

**Table 13. World Bank Industry Lending for Four South Asian Countries, by Purpose of Loan, Fiscal Years 1971–90**
Millions of U.S. dollars

| Purpose of loan | India | Pakistan | Bangladesh | Sri Lanka |
|---|---|---|---|---|
| Specific project loans | 2,198.8 | 216.5 | 181.5 | 0.0 |
| Fertilizers | 1,598.8 | 183.5 | 106.0 | 0.0 |
| Petrochemicals and refineries | 500.0 | 33.0 | 75.5 | 0.0 |
| Paper and pulp | 100.0 | 0.0 | 0.0 | 0.0 |
| | | | | |
| Rehabilitation and restructuring | 500.0 | 96.0 | 95.0 | 0.0 |
| Cement | 500.0 | 96.0 | 0.0 | 0.0 |
| Textiles | 0.0 | 0.0 | 75.0 | 0.0 |
| Jute | 0.0 | 0.0 | 20.0 | 0.0 |
| | | | | |
| DFIs:[a] general purpose | 585.0 | 400.0 | 75.0 | 112.8 |
| | | | | |
| DFIs:[a] specific purpose | 1,380.0 | 204.0 | 78.4 | 54.5 |
| SSEs[a] | 65.0 | 134.0 | 42.0 | 50.0 |
| Export development | 545.0 | 70.0 | 25.0 | 4.5 |
| Technology development | 560.0 | 0.0 | 0.0 | 0.0 |
| Electronics | 210.0 | 0.0 | 0.0 | 0.0 |
| Energy conservation | 0.0 | 0.0 | 11.4 | 0.0 |
| | | | | |
| Sectoral reform | 0.0 | 300.0 | 175.0 | 0.0 |
| Financial sector | 0.0 | 150.0 | 175.0 | 0.0 |
| Industrial sector | 0.0 | 150.0 | 0.0 | 0.0 |
| | | | | |
| Total | 4,663.8 | 1,216.5 | 604.9 | 167.3 |

Source: World Bank, *Annual Report,* various years.
a. DFI = development financing institution; SSE = small-scale enterprise.

prises in this field, and the Indian government took a restrictive approach to allowing private investment in the sector. As part of the Bank's policy dialogue with India, an understanding was reached around the mid-1960s: the Bank would lend for fertilizer units in the public sector, while India would open the field for private investment. Between 1971 and 1986 the Bank made twelve loans in India for fertilizer projects, for a total of $1,598.8 million: eight operations in the public sector ($788 million) and four ($811 million) for plants implemented by the Indian Farmers Fertilizers Cooperative (IFFCO) in the cooperative sector.[22] Earlier loans, during the years 1972–75, were for plants based on fuel oil or naphtha as feedstock, whereas those in the late 1980s included loans for natural-gas-based plants fed by pipeline from the Bombay

High field. Inasmuch as the Bank has also assisted gas development and conveyance from Bombay High, its overall support to India's fertilizer development has been substantial; the Bank has, indeed, played a major role in India's becoming the fourth-largest producer of fertilizers in the world.

In the earlier loans, delays ranging between one and two years and substantial cost overruns resulted from delays on the part of both suppliers and executing agencies. In some cases teething problems have also been serious. Problems such as equipment failures, power shortages, poor quality and erratic supply of feedstock, and managerial and labor problems have occurred from time to time. However, a detailed study by the Bank found that all except one of the projects had achieved capacity utilization of around 80 percent in the mid-1980s and were economically viable.[23] Many of the implementation problems in the fertilizer sector in India could be traced to India's insistence on maximizing domestic supplies and engineering services, a policy that has not been without its dividends: in the words of a Bank study, "this strategy of learning to cope with a multitude of operational as well as design problems led to the formation of a highly skilled cadre of technical and operational staff which provides the basis for a rapid expansion of the subsector" and in turn "has created numerous opportunities to use domestic capabilities."

The Bank has not always seen eye-to-eye with India in choosing technology. Differences on this score came to a head in the Thal Vaishet project, where the government revised an earlier choice (which had been objectively arrived at) to favor an equipment supplier (Snamprogetti) that had not been on the original short list. The government claimed standardization of technology as the justification, but the Bank was not convinced and decided not to render the loan effective.[24] In the longer run this technological tie-up has resulted in high-cost contractual arrangements for process know-how and equipment in Indian fertilizer projects.

In the late 1980s the Bank took a pause in what had been its continued lending for individual projects and turned its attention to the sectoral problems of the Indian fertilizer industry. An important Bank study in 1987 found that, apart from a small group of public sector plants of earlier vintage, which were noncompetitive because of very high energy costs and low capacity utilization, capital costs were so high in second-generation gas-based plants as to undermine economic viability despite very favorable energy and conversion factors.[25] The reasons were mainly threefold: technological tie-ups, which limited competitive contractual arrangements for design, technology, and equipment; high costs of domestic equipment and supplies used in projects; and a retention price scheme (RPS) that encouraged overcapitalization by failing to provide incentives for cost optimization.

Based on this analysis, the Bank's policy reform package consists of two main elements. One is to mothball and, if necessary, retire the unviable plants, and the other is to replace the RPS with a pricing regime calculated to bring investment and operating costs, in the longer run, in line with or at least closer to international parameters. Since high prices for fertilizers in India are largely a reflection of high production costs, this strategy, if implemented, will also help to reduce fertilizer subsidies to farmers and will make an important contribution to reducing the government's budget deficit. The Bank has been able to press its dialogue on pricing reform along similar lines in Pakistan and Bangladesh, where, however, domestic production is of a much smaller proportion. It remains to be seen whether it will succeed in India, where the reforms envisaged will entail high political costs as a result of layoffs as well as short-run disincentives for new investment and expansion.

In Pakistan an early Bank loan (1968) was for a joint venture between the Dawood Industrial Group and Hercules, Inc., a U.S. company. This was successful at implementation and in subsequent stages. Later loans were for the Multan fertilizer project (a joint venture of the government and Abu Dhabi National Oil Company) and for the Fauji project (implemented by a private charitable trust for ex-servicemen). The Multan project experienced a large cost overrun due to a sharp escalation in imported and domestic costs and force majeure circumstances such as flooding, shipping accidents, and political disturbances. Production in this plant has, however, stabilized, and good capacity utilization has been achieved. Both implementation and production performance have been satisfactory in the Fauji project. There the Bank made an important contribution by identifying a second technical partner to replace the first one, who withdrew soon after project approval, and to restitute the initial loan. In Bangladesh the Bank has financed the gas-based project in Ashuganj and the rehabilitation of three other major plants.

The Bank has made a significant contribution to the development of the petrochemical industry in India in lending to the public sector Indian Petrochemical Corporation ($500 million in two loans). Refinery improvement loans in India, Pakistan, and Bangladesh have contributed to better capacity utilization, rationalization of production, and energy conservation.

DEVELOPMENT FINANCING INSTITUTIONS. In India the principal DFI through which the Bank has operated is the Industrial Credit and Investment Corporation of India (ICICI).[26] Up to 1981 the Bank had made thirteen general-purpose loans to the ICICI to meet the equipment import requirements of large and medium-size industries. Since then the Bank's approach has been, on the one hand, to target its lines of credit more closely to specific industries and purposes (SSEs, exports, technology development, electronics, energy conservation) and, on the other, to diversify on-lending through multiple intermediaries including commercial banks, to ensure better coverage in terms of regions, industries, and types of entrepreneurs and to facilitate the negotiation of comprehensive financial packages. In this phase as well, the ICICI has been a major participant in on-lending.

The ICICI has been consistently commended in the Bank's evaluations as a "sound, mature, and efficiently managed institution."[27] Through the years the ICICI has progressed on many fronts. Whereas its portfolio originally tended to be concentrated in western India, it is now more regionally diversified, with special attention being given to backward areas. Rates of return, repayment ratios, and disbursement profiles have been satisfactory. Good capability has been built up in project identification and in loan appraisals, monitoring, and evaluation. The institution has succeeded in diversifying its foreign exchange sources by tapping commercial loans in international markets at low spreads. Government ownership since 1969 has not impaired the ICICI's autonomy. To all this the Bank's close and cordial interaction with the ICICI has contributed a great deal.

The Bank's involvement in the Industrial Development Bank of India (IDBI), a public sector institution, has been much more limited, dating only from the 1970s; previously the Bank had lent only to private sector DFIs. In recent years the IDBI has participated, along with the ICICI and other participating financial institutions, in lines of credit for electronics and export industries and for technology development. It has also provided a channel for on-lending to state financial corporations (SFCs) in India for small and medium-size industries and for public sector and joint ventures in the states. Because of policy differences with the government regarding subsidies and levels of protection, the Bank has not extended any specific lines of credit to SSEs in India. Nor has its second-best approach of supporting SSEs through SFCs been sustained or successful; SFCs have had high arrearage ratios, and their management, never very strong, has been subject to frequent political interference.

In Pakistan, the PICIC (Pakistan Industrial Credit and Investment Corporation) corresponds to the ICICI in being the Bank's chosen vehicle for intermediation. The PICIC's portfolio underwent major shocks in the 1970s, which witnessed such disruptive political and economic developments as the civil war, the external hostilities of 1971, and the nationalization of major industries. Very large arrears from its borrowers have been a major problem for the PICIC. Beginning in about the mid-1980s, the Bank has diversified its intermediaries in Pakistan, relying much more on the commercial banking sector for general-purpose lending and for supporting reforms in the financial and industrial sectors. To a limited extent the Bank has also used public sector DFIs in Pakistan, namely, the Industrial Development Bank of Pakistan (IDBP) and the National Development Finance Corporation (NDFC), which finances public enterprises. The IDBP's portfolio has been adversely affected by sizable arrears in repayment, besides a serious loss in its portfolio and professional staff consequent on the separation of Bangladesh. Political interference has also been a problem.

The Bank's experience with the Bangladesh Shilpa Bank (BSB) has been bedeviled with problems right from the beginning. Over a long period, arrears have affected 90 percent or more of the portfolio, management has been subject to political interference both in lending and in effecting recoveries, and loans have been heavily concentrated in Dhaka and Chittagong. By the mid-1980s the Bank had decided to discontinue further lending to the BSB until it made tangible progress in restructuring its portfolio and improving its creditworthiness. An action plan toward this end was prepared, and the Bank's financial sector loan to Bangladesh in 1990 was addressed, inter alia, to promoting the needed changes. The question has been raised in the Bank's PPARs whether in retrospect it would not have been advisable for the Bank to have "conditioned support for BSB to actual institutional and policy reforms and not to mere assurances of prospective initiatives and actions."[28]

In Sri Lanka all the Bank's lending for the industrial sector has been in the form of loans intermediated through the Development Finance Corporation of Ceylon (DFCC) and other public financing institutions. Although the bulk has been for medium-size and large industries in the private sector, loans to SSEs have also been significant. The DFCC has been rated as a successful institution overall, and the Bank has been generally satisfied with its competence in loan management and in mobilizing external and domestic resources.

### Agriculture

Agriculture has been, along with energy, a leading sector in the Bank's project lending operations in South Asia, claiming about 29 percent of cumulative lending up to fiscal year 1990. There was a sharp increase in the sector's share from about 19 percent in the pre-1970 period to nearly 39 percent in the 1970s, followed by a decline to about 26 percent in the 1980s. In broad terms, Bank projects in the last two decades have sought to support the spread of new technology (the so-called Green Revolution) through the provision of irrigation, credit, and extension services; to diversify crop husbandry with allied activities (agro-industries, dairying, fisheries, and perennial or tree crops); and to pay heed to problems of resource management (of forests and watersheds, for instance) and regional balance (area development).

The subsectoral pattern of lending during the 1971–90 period to the major South Asian borrowers is shown in table 14. In all countries irrigation accounts for the single largest share within the agricultural portfolio: about 47 percent in the region as a whole and about 40 to 50 percent in the major countries. Among other subsectors, agricultural credit dominates (19 percent) but is almost entirely concentrated in India and Pakistan. Area development is significant in Bangladesh and Sri Lanka and tree crops in Sri Lanka. Research and extension have received attention in all countries. The only sector loan has gone to Pakistan. The discussion that follows is confined to the important subsectors of concentration in the four major borrowers.

IRRIGATION. Although irrigation has had a long history in India, it is only since independence that its development has been striking and sustained. Net irrigated area has doubled from 21 million hectares in 1950 to 42 million hectares by the mid-1980s, with gross irrigated area rising from 23 million to 54 million hectares in the same period. Concurrently there has been a considerable regional diversification, especially into previously unirrigated parts of central (Rajasthan and Madhya Pradesh) and eastern (Bihar and Orissa) India; an enormous increase in private well irrigation, which has trebled and now accounts for nearly half of total net irrigated area; and a reorientation of irrigation from extensive water use for drought protection toward intensive application to achieve productivity increases.

The development of irrigation since the 1950s has thrown up a number of priorities and interrelated problems. There have been competing claims on overall resources between capital investments and maintenance outlays, and within the investment budget between new starts and completion of ongoing projects. There is a need to close the gap between creation of potential and its utilization and to increase efficiency and equity through reliable supply and better water management by users. Distribution of water between different types of users, crops, and seasons should be more equitable. Dams should be of better construction quality and built to higher standards of safety. Public sector capabilities in project identification and preparation, construction, supervision,

**Table 14. World Bank Agriculture Lending for Four South Asian Countries, by Purpose of Loan, Fiscal Years 1970–91**
Millions of U.S. dollars

| Purpose of loan | India | Pakistan | Bangladesh | Sri Lanka |
|---|---|---|---|---|
| Irrigation, flood control, and drainage | 4,324.0 (47.0) | 778.1 (44.6) | 499.9 (53.0) | 203.1 (36.6) |
| Agricultural credit | 1,887.4 (20.5) | 457.8 (26.2) | 40.0 (4.2) | 0.0 (0.0) |
| Agricultural sector lending | 0.0 (0.0) | 200.0 (11.5) | 0.0 (0.0) | 0.0 (0.0) |
| Agro-industry | 898.0 (9.8) | 106.4 (6.1) | 52.5 (5.6) | 0.0 (0.0) |
| Area development | 539.2 (5.9) | 17.0 (1.0) | 141.0 (15.0) | 76.5 (13.8) |
| Fisheries | 55.5 (0.6) | 1.7 (0.1) | 72.6 (7.7) | 0.0 (0.0) |
| Forestry | 349.8 (3.8) | 21.0 (1.2) | 39.0 (4.1) | 28.9 (5.2) |
| Livestock | 584.1 (6.3) | 10.0 (0.6) | 0.0 (0.0) | 47.0 (8.5) |
| Perennial crops | 84.0 (0.9) | 0.0 (0.0) | 21.0 (2.2) | 165.0 (29.8) |
| Research and extension | 480.2 (5.2) | 153.2 (8.7) | 75.6 (8.2) | 34.1 (6.1) |
| Total | 9,202.2 (100.0) | 1,745.2 (100.0) | 941.6 (100.0) | 554.6 (100.0) |

Source: World Bank, *Annual Report,* various years. Figures in parentheses are percentages of column totals.

operation, and maintenance require improvement. There should be more effective response to environmental issues, especially the resettlement and rehabilitation of displaced persons. Adequate attention should be paid to economic rates of return in the choice of projects and to better cost recovery to ensure the financial sustainability of investments.[29]

The Bank has attempted to respond to this gamut of problems in the choice and structuring of its projects and through its technical assistance and policy dialogue. The latter have been addressed mainly to issues such as command area development, canal lining, on-farm development, structures and practices to facilitate better water management, dam safety, resettlement and rehabilitation, training, and cost recovery. Success in achieving these objectives has, however, been below expectations. The most commonly noticed implementation deficiencies in Bank projects are delays and cost overruns, reduced command areas, and lower productivity impact.

There is much evidence in supervision reports, project completion reports (PCRs), PPARs, and sector reviews to indicate that project design has often been based on incomplete data and field investigations. In a number of cases appraisal preceded the completion of detailed designs. In some, more cost-effective alternatives were not explored in project choice or design. In others, inappropriate sequencing of works has been the problem. Funding for time-slice and sectoral investments, while promoting flexible and fast disbursement, has paid insufficient attention to technical soundness and economic viability.[30] Inadequate budgetary allocations and delayed releases of funds on the part of executing agencies have been a major cause of delays and cost overruns. Managerial problems have included shortages and high turnover of key staff, inadequate coordination, and poor supervision of contractors. Shortages of cement, steel, and equipment have also been fairly common.

On the environmental aspects of irrigation projects, the two major areas in which the Bank has concentrated are dam safety and resettlement and rehabilitation of displaced families. The Bank's efforts have resulted in greater awareness of and improved procedures for dam safety, and in the funding of a few specific projects. The record in resettlement and rehabilitation has been much less satisfactory. A review of twenty-two projects funded between 1978 and 1990 that entailed resettlement concluded that "in several key projects, despite legal covenants, the resettlement component has yet to be prepared, or is being implemented either inadequately or not at all."[31]

Resettlement and environmental issues became a cause célèbre in the Narmada project in Gujarat, for which the Bank made two loans totaling $450 million in 1985.[32] Widespread opposition to the project from environmental groups in India and in the United States prevailed upon the Bank to appoint an independent review of the resettlement and environmental aspects of the project in June 1991 by a team under Bradford Morse, former head of the UNDP. The review, published in June 1992, was the first independent assessment of a major project. It concluded that the Bank and India both failed to carry out adequate assessments of the human impacts and environmental consequences of the projects and that the measures instituted or implemented to mitigate them were far from adequate.

The report documented several specific failures. There was inadequate assessment of the human impact before funding in 1985. Planners failed to consult the affected population, resulting in hostility to the project, which created serious obstacles to implementation. The claims of several categories of affected families, such as members of indigenous tribes, squatters, landless families, canal-displaced marginal farmers, and elder sons in affected households, were ignored. Relief efforts in the states of Maharashtra and Madhya Pradesh, where the bulk of the affected people live, were inadequate in scale and poorly implemented. There was a lack of data and programs for tackling the environmental impact—upstream, downstream, and in the command area—particularly in regard to catchment treatment, health hazards, and the impact on fisheries.

According to the review, the failure of the Bank was a consequence of its incremental strategy: "The Bank has been aware of major resettlement problems . . . but has failed to act firmly to address them. Violations of legal covenants are flagged and then forgotten; conditions are imposed and when the borrower fails to meet them, the conditions are relaxed or their deadlines are postponed." Since this strategy has not yielded results and has been counterproductive in provoking the intense hostility of the affected population (supported by activists), the review recommended that the Bank "take a step back" from the projects and consider them afresh.

In response to the review, the Bank admitted "that past efforts—including efforts by the Bank—to resolve" the long-standing problems identified in the Narmada project "have not been adequate."[33] A detailed action plan was formulated in collaboration with the Indian government to remedy the various deficiencies. On this basis the Bank decided to continue its support for the project. However, this incremental step also failed to help. The Indian government was unable to meet the requirements of the action plan and eventually withdrew the project from Bank funding.

As in the case of environmental issues, the incremental strategy of the Bank has not succeeded in upgrading cost recovery. Cost recovery covenants in individual project agreements have been "seldom enforced, often relaxed and sometimes ignored," and the Bank's standard response has been to provide for further studies, which has enabled an "easy way out."[34] Despite its substantial lending for irrigation, rural electrification, and tubewells (the latter being the main component in its agricultural credit portfolio), the Bank has been unable or unwilling, or both, to pursue effectively the issue of large and mounting subsidies—for surface irrigation and groundwater exploitation through electrified pumpsets—which now add up to about two-thirds of all farm subsidies in India.

In Pakistan the Bank's involvement in irrigation falls into three distinct phases. In the 1950s the Bank was preoccupied with the negotiation of the Indus Waters treaty between India and Pakistan.[35] Investments beginning in the 1960s related to the large Indus Basin works arising from the treaty, namely, the Mangla and Tarbela dams and major barrages and canals connected with them. It was only in the 1970s and 1980s that the Bank was able to concentrate on the long-standing problems of waterlogging and salinity in Pakistan's irrigation system.[36] In doing so it was greatly influenced by approaches evolved by the U.S. Agency for International Development (USAID) in earlier decades, when the Bank itself was preoccupied with Indus Basin works.

Beginning with the first USAID-initiated SCARP (salinity control and reclamation project) in 1958, the preferred technical option was vertical drainage (the use of tubewells to pump excess water into canals) based on public tubewells rather than horizontal drainage (lining of canals to reduce seepage, surface-tiled drains, and subsurface drains) and private tubewell development. The Bank went along with this approach and made three SCARP-type loans during the 1970s. Although these projects led to investments in a large number of public tubewells, they had no appreciable impact on the incidence and extent of waterlogging and salinity. A number of technical and managerial problems relating to SCARP tubewells also began to assert themselves, such as mismanagement, frequent pump breakdowns, electricity failures, and high recurring costs, with declining ratios of cost recovery.

It was only during the late 1970s that the Bank began to entertain serious reservations about this model. The change of course finally came in its revised action program (RAP) of 1979, which emphasized smaller system rehabilitation and water management projects and reliance on private tubewells, especially in nonsaline areas. Bank lending in the 1980s, following this approach, has been for a series of rehabilitation, drainage, and on-farm management projects emphasizing horizontal drainage and water conservation in the field. A major individual drainage project has been funded in Sind (the Left Bank Canal).

A part of the irrigation portfolio has included loans from time to time (1977, 1987, and 1988) for the repair and rehabilitation of flood-damaged irrigation works. The Bank has also provided technical assistance and institutional inputs to the Water and Power Development Authority (WAPDA). In the late 1980s a project was undertaken to phase out public tubewells by transferring them to private ownership. In effect, the technical philosophy of the Bank's irrigation lending to Pakistan in the 1980s represents a complete reversal of that followed during most of the 1970s.

The Bank has been more successful in Pakistan than in India in improving cost recovery in irrigation. Water charges have been raised on successive occasions during the 1980s, and the government has accepted the objective of full cost recovery in principle. However, maintenance outlays continue to be underfunded by the provincial governments, which are the ones responsible for it, with the consequence that considerable new funding is periodically required for repair and restoration. The drain on resources entailed by public tubewells has been another factor in exacerbating the resource problem.

Overall, waterlogging and salinity continue to be serious problems in Pakistan, and their solution will depend much on microlevel research, technology, and management. In this context the Bank has been criticized for tending to rely far too much on the shifting predilections of external consultants and for having failed to promote domestic capacity in WAPDA and elsewhere for location-specific, problem-oriented action research in tackling Pakistan's persistent problems of waterlogging, drainage, and salinity.[37]

Irrigation projects in Bangladesh have faced different problems. Bangladesh is blessed with massive water resources and burdened with massive problems of water control. Annual flows in the Brahmaputra-Ganges river system are about double those of the Mississippi and six times those of the Indus. In July and August, the peak of the wet season (April–November), flooding usually occurs when snowmelt runoff and monsoon rains coincide, submerging about two-thirds of cultivated land to varying depths. During the dry season (December–March) there is little rainfall, and about 60 percent of cultivable land remains fallow. This is particularly unfortunate because dry-season irrigation for the Boro rice crop has proved to be the more important contributor to incremental grain production. At the same time, Bangladesh is endowed with enormous groundwater aquifers, sustained by a highly dependable natural recharge cycle, which have been only partially exploited for dry-season cultivation.

Complex issues relating to technical and economic options and trade-offs and priorities for flood control and irrigation in Bangladesh have been debated over the years.[38] In the early 1960s a master plan prepared by the UNDP emphasized what it saw as long-term solutions to the flooding problem through constructing embankments and polders to prevent inundation. As these projects were implemented, the validity of this approach came to be questioned from a number of angles. The structural works were difficult to engineer, extremely costly, susceptible to damage from the changing course of the river, and expensive to maintain, and they utilized scarce arable land. Nor was it easy to combine wet-season irrigation objectives with flood control measures. It proved infeasible to link cost recoveries to flood control, while the limited recoveries from irrigation were inadequate in relation to the large outlays required to ensure against floods.

A major Land and Water Resources (LWR) Sector Study undertaken by the Bank in 1972 represented a shift from the approach of the UNDP master plan and essentially came out in favor of larger-scale surface irrigation requiring primary pumping, minor surface irrigation from natural drains using low-lift pumps, and groundwater utilization by means of a variety of tubewells: deep, shallow, and hand-operated. Flood control and drainage works were to be limited to relatively modest and localized investments that could be expected to be cost-effective. These broad priorities have influenced the Bank's lending strategies in the 1970s and 1980s.

Lending for minor irrigation has been accomplished through the Bangladesh Agricultural Development Corporation (BADC). The BADC had been renting out irrigation equipment, mostly low-lift pumps and deep tubewells, to farmers' irrigation groups or cooperatives before 1981; since then it has moved to outright sales and to a greater emphasis on shallow tubewells. Although minor irrigation has, in principle, sought to promote more equitable water use, the operations of the BADC have raised a number of problems, to which the Bank's and the government's responses have been neither clear nor consistent. The problems include how to reduce subsidies in the pricing and rentals of equipment; determining the appropriate pace of transition from rentals to sales; improving the maintenance and utilization of equipment; and establishing a greater role for the private sector in the manufacture, supply, and servicing of equipment.[39] Critics, within and outside the Bank, have pointed out that benefits from minor irrigation projects have been highly skewed in favor of larger landowners, who have dominated irrigation groups and cooperatives. These landowners have preempted supplies and services to themselves and acted as "waterlords," selling water at high prices to small and marginal farmers and tenants.[40] Although the shift to privatization-cum-sales has enlarged the clientele for pumpsets and tubewells, it has also had the effect of restricting the access of smaller cultivators to them. Groundwater regulation, which the Bank sought to promote in its earlier lending operations, has had perverse effects on equity: large farmers, who were early entrants and major beneficiaries from lending, have installed deep tubewells, but regulation has discouraged small farmers seeking to install shallow tubewells. The Bank has come, somewhat belatedly, to the conclusion that groundwater regulation is neither feasible nor desirable.

Meanwhile the catastrophic floods that affected Bangladesh in 1987 and in 1988, displacing some 30 million people from their homes, once again brought the unresolved problem of flood control to the fore. Following these floods as many as four major studies were sponsored by the UNDP, USAID, and the governments of France and Japan in the late 1980s. At the request of the Bangladesh aid group the Bank has tried to sift through, prioritize, and phase in the proposals that emerged from those studies, arbitrating between large structures on the one hand and more affordable measures on the other. The Action Plan for Flood Control that was under consideration in 1989 included nonstructural measures (flood forecasting, warning, preparedness, and disaster management); structural protection (embankments, drainage, water control), with special emphasis on protecting urban concentrations; and regionwide project-oriented studies. An agenda is thus being evolved in Bangladesh for flood control and irrigation, largely as a result of trial and error over a period of nearly three decades. The action plan can be expected to generate a portfolio of domestic projects for flood control, but regional projects to tame and utilize the eastern waters of the Ganges, the Brahmaputra, and their tributaries and branches are also a major challenge. If the Bank is someday able to promote a basinwide approach in this matter among India, Nepal, and Bangladesh, it could once again play a historic role, recalling its signal contribution to the Indus Basin settlement in the 1950s.[41]

From an irrigation perspective, Sri Lanka is divided distinctly into wet and dry zones. The wet zone, located in the southwestern part of the island, occupies about 30 percent of its land area but accounts for more than 80 percent of cultivated land. Extension of irrigation in the dry zone is, accordingly, a major priority. The Mahaweli Development Master Plan developed in 1965–68 seeks to provide irrigation to about 365,000 hectares of land in the dry zone through fifteen reservoirs located on the Mahaweli Ganga River and its tributaries and on the Madura Oya River, and to generate 500 MW of power. The original plan was divided in three phases to be implemented over thirty years. Although the Bank showed some initial interest in the project, it did not play an active role in the studies leading to the master plan because of the deterioration in its relations with the Sri Lanka Freedom Party (SLFP) government of 1961–65. The studies were then carried out by UNDP and the Food and Agriculture Organization (FAO). The Bank's first loan to the project was for the initial stage of the first phase. It included components for a power station and for downstream development of irrigation. Despite a delay of two years in completion, this project was judged successful on the whole, the main problems that remained being cost recovery, effective water management, and illegal occupation of land.

Late in 1977 the United National Party (UNP) government then in power decided to accelerate the Mahaweli development program. At this stage the Bank was much more forthcoming—indeed, uncharacteristically so—and in fact willing to offer a loan even before the completion of an implementation strategy study it had earlier insisted upon. The main reasons for this were strong pressure from bilateral lenders, the Bank's own desire not to be left out of a prestigious project, and its interest in supporting the right-of-center UNP government, which saw acceleration of the Mahaweli program as a compensation for the sociopolitical costs of the food subsidy reductions, devaluation, and liberalization. Starting again in 1977, the Bank by 1984 had made three more project loans and a technical assistance loan for Mahaweli. Total lending for Mahaweli in the four project loans (1970–84) amounted to $183.6 million, and the project has dominated Bank lending for irrigation in Sri Lanka.

At the macroeconomic level the accelerated Mahaweli program has inflicted severe costs on the Sri Lankan economy. The high and escalating cost of the program (from 12 billion to 40 billion rupees by the mid-1980s) led to substantial budget deficits in the early 1980s and consequent domestic inflation and balance of payments problems. Mahaweli has also diverted construction materials and capacity from other projects. Through its initial hesitancy (in the late 1960s) and its subsequent enthusiasm (since 1977), the Bank has not put itself in a position to moderate the destabilizing effects of this mammoth project on the rest of Sri Lanka's economy.[42]

The Bank's dialogue with the Sri Lanka government over cost recovery in irrigation projects has had a checkered course. Cost recovery covenants in earlier projects, including the one in the first Mahaweli loan, had to be renegotiated when the SLFP came to power in 1970 because the free delivery of water to farmers was one of its election promises. At that point the Bank settled for promises of "future" cost recoveries based on further studies. In fact, no water charges were levied from 1970 to 1977. The UNP government, which came to power in 1977, tried to introduce water charges in 1978, but collections ceased in 1981. Following the negotiations for the third Mahaweli loan, collections began again in 1984. They are reported to have reached reasonable levels in the Mahaweli system but have remained negligible elsewhere.

AGRICULTURAL CREDIT. Following the report of a joint reconnaissance mission with the FAO in 1968, the Bank energetically entered into indirect "wholesale" lending for provision of agricultural credits to farmers in India, with individual loans during 1970–73 to ten major states for a total amount of $637 million. Thereafter, on the basis of its experience at the state level, the Bank moved to mediate its lending through the Agricultural Refinance and Development Corporation (ARDC, later to become NABARD, the National Bank for Agriculture and Rural Development). Between 1975 and 1986 five lines of credit for a total of $1,250 million were extended to the ARDC and NABARD, which in turn have used cooperative credit institutions at the state and substate levels for on-lending. Minor irrigation projects (open dug wells, tubewells, and electric pumpsets) have been the main component in agricultural credit financing. Earlier loans also allowed some measure of financing for land leveling and tractors, whereas later loans routed through the ARDC and NABARD covered supplementary activities such as livestock, fisheries, poultry, tree crops, and horticulture.

Besides providing a useful conduit for substantial resource transfers through large loans, the Bank's decision in the mid-1970s to channel its lending for agricultural credit through a "wholesaling" institution at the national level has had several advantages. The ARDC and later NABARD have been able to reach out to less developed states and regions (whose share has improved over time to 50 percent) and to small farmers (who account for nearly half of all borrowers) and to allocate funds to different states according to their needs and performance. Bank loans have contributed to improved procedures and standards within the on-lending agencies. Working with these institutions, the Bank has been able to strengthen state groundwater directorates and to suggest regulations to prevent excessive groundwater exploitation. Commercial banks have been induced to supplement the cooperative credits.

Although the objectives and the modality of lending in this subsector have thus been sound, severe institutional problems have emerged over time in India's agricultural credit system. These relate primarily to overdues and to inadequate lending margins, which in combination have begun to gravely threaten the viability of the cooperative credit system. At the close of the 1980s, 40 to 50 percent of agricultural loans had fallen overdue, and a sizable proportion of these were in default for over three years. Apart from the standard reasons that explain low recovery (such as variable incomes of borrowers, poor project selection, and inadequate follow-up), political interference in the form of promises to write off loans or to waive interest dues have encouraged willful default, mainly on the part of larger farmers.

NABARD has sought to deal with the problem of mounting overdues by cutting off refinancing to cooperative banks or their branches with high proportions of defaulted loans in their portfolios; this, however, has only limited the availability of credit, mainly to small and first-time borrowers. The second major problem is that lending margins, the spread between on-lending and refinance rates of interest, have been kept at levels (about 3 percent) that are only about half of what is required to cover the costs of administration and normal risks. In effect, therefore, there is a significant interest subsidy to the ultimate borrowers in addition to the subsidy implied when borrowers default or have their debt-servicing obligations waived.[43]

Successive PPARs relating to the second (1977), third (1980), and fourth (1982) ARDC loans drew attention to the unsustainable level of arrearages. Performance of the third ARDC loan was actually classified as unsatisfactory because of the large and growing volume of arrears. The PPAR for that loan, issued in 1989, wondered "whether meeting the short-run disbursement targets of the Bank and the government's need for foreign exchange . . . was adequate justification for continuing to support a deteriorating institutional credit system in India."[44] The alarm bell was sounded too late, however, for meanwhile, in 1986, the Bank had made one more loan, on this occasion to NABARD. All that was done to address the problem of arrearages was to provide that a comprehensive study would be undertaken to formulate measures to rectify the situation. There has been no further lending to NABARD while the study is being completed. When, on what scale, and subject to what reforms—actual or promised—lending for agricultural credit will resume remains to be seen. The Bank, of course, cannot be blamed for poor recoveries. But it can be reasonably criticized for not trying hard enough to see that credit discipline is enforced in a timely manner, and it can certainly be faulted for continuing to lend in the face of a deteriorating situation, allowing resource transfer considerations to prevail over concerns for institutional sustainability.

Certain other issues related to agricultural lending are also important. There has been an intense debate on the labor displacement effects of lending for the purchase of tractors (see the discussion with reference to Pakistan below).[45] In practical terms, however, this is not a major issue in India because of the relatively small proportion of lending for mechanization. Another concern relates to the overuse of groundwater and the need for groundwater regulation. The

Bank has tried to promote groundwater discipline through spacing and density criteria for wells, but no state in India has been able or willing, for political reasons, to bring forward comprehensive legislation in this respect. Highly subsidized agricultural power tariffs are an added factor in the wasteful use of water (and electricity). The Bank has provided substantial support to both power and well irrigation and could have attempted a cross-sectoral aggregation of leverage on the subsidy issue. That the opportunity was missed is regrettable for several reasons: cheap power has mainly benefited larger farmers and has led to ecologically undesirable levels and patterns of groundwater use, and it is the single most important factor responsible for the poor financial position of the state electricity boards.

In Pakistan lending for agricultural credit has all along been routed through the Agricultural Development Bank of Pakistan (ADBP). Three loans in this area were made from 1965 through the end of the 1960s, but a long lull in operations followed until 1980. This interruption was due to the poor management and recovery performance of ADBP, for which political interference was partly responsible. ADBP improved recoveries in the 1970s, enabling the Bank to make a new series of loans, for larger amounts, in the 1980s. Unlike NABARD in India, ADBP has continued to maintain a reasonably good recovery record.

A substantial part of agricultural lending in Pakistan has gone into financing of farm mechanization, principally tractors. Tractors have resulted in increased production, mainly through expansion of cultivated area rather than higher cropping intensities, shifts in cropping patterns, or yield increases. Large farmers have been the primary beneficiaries from access to finance as well as subsidized interest rates, which ADBP has been able to ensure because of its low-interest borrowing from the State Bank of Pakistan. On the other hand, tractors have led to displacement of tenants, casualization of farm labor, and an increase in disguised, if not in open, unemployment. As noted above, there has been a debate within the Bank and outside on these socially regressive effects of tractors, but the Bank has tended to underplay the issue and to go along with the government and ADBP in their continued support for tractorization.[46]

A much smaller proportion of agricultural lending through ADBP has been for groundwater irrigation. This is surprising because the irrigation strategies of the Bank have emphasized the role of private tubewells in the control of waterlogging, and tubewells, unlike tractors, have a positive effect on labor absorption. The main criticisms of the Bank's agricultural lending in Pakistan thus relate to both commission and omission: tractor loans have run counter to professed equity objectives of employment promotion in rural areas, while inadequate lending for tubewells points to lack of coordination in lending strategies between the irrigation and agricultural credit subsectors.

AGRICULTURAL EXTENSION. The agricultural extension projects of the Bank represent an ambitious effort at reforming grass-roots agricultural administration in India, a country of vast size, diversity, and complexity of farming conditions. At the time of the Bank's initial involvement in the mid-1970s, agricultural extension services in India suffered from several shortcomings: poorly trained and inadequate staff fragmented among different crops, channels of command, and types of duties; weak linkages between extension and research; and inadequate allocations of finance and manpower for extension. Basing its strategy on pilot projects in the Chambal and Rajasthan command areas, the Bank made fifteen loans for agricultural extension in India between 1977 and 1987, covering as many as seventeen states. Earlier loans were for individual states, but those since 1985 have each covered a number of states.

The Bank's blueprint for extension is based on what is called the training-and-visit (T&V) approach.[47] Although eminently sensible in its conception, this approach has suffered much distortion in both design and implementation across the several states of India. The problems include high turnover, poor training, and low motivation of staff; diversion of extension staff to nonextension duties; inadequate tuning of extension messages to local cropping conditions and farmers' resources; poor links with research, inadequate research inputs, and feeble reciprocal feedback between field and research; deficient selection of contact farmers and lack of interest on their part in dissemination; and inadequate coordination between extension and availability of inputs. The Bank itself has been criticized for taking on too much at too rapid a pace and for replicating a single model over states and regions with very different administrative and agroeconomic conditions instead of stabilizing implementation in a few states and systematically incorporating lessons from earlier phases into subsequent ones.

There has been a vigorous debate between the Bank and its critics regarding the extent of these problems and the degree to which they have continued in different states.[48] The Bank has tried to effect improvements in its repeat projects in some of the states and has carried out detailed reviews, resulting in a number of specific recommendations to strengthen the functioning of the system. The limited number of studies evaluating the T&V approach are not conclusive, for it is difficult to disaggregate the impact of extension on agricultural productivity from changes in other factors such as irrigation, credit availability, fertilizer use, and prices.

In Pakistan, Bangladesh, and Sri Lanka T&V has been promoted on a much smaller scale. In Pakistan, beginning with smaller operations between 1978 and 1985, a substantial loan was made for the introduction of T&V in Punjab and Sind in 1987. Initial experience has been more or less the same as in India,with high staff turnover and other managerial problems. It is too soon to say whether the Punjab-Sind project will be able to overcome these problems. In Sri Lanka as well, the problems encountered in India and Pakistan have repeated themselves.

AREA DEVELOPMENT. An early project, approved in 1974, provided five-year time-slice financing for India's Drought Prone Areas Program (DPAP), which at that time covered seventy-two districts in thirteen states. This was conceived as a pilot project through which project components could be tested and the successful ones introduced in larger scale subsequent operations. The project scope was wide-ranging, including water resources, dry land farming, fodder and livestock, forestry, fisheries, sericulture, horticulture, and technical assistance. Although the project itself was a reasonable success, it did not fulfill its function as a pilot because the monitoring and evaluation component was not implemented; thus no systematic lessons could be learned for the future. More important, the government did not request further Bank participation in the DPAP.

Other area development projects in India in the 1970s were mostly directed toward the utilization of irrigation in specified command areas (Chambal command in Madhya Pradesh, for example) by providing supplementary investments (field channels, roads) and inputs (credit, extension services). In the 1980s the orientation of area development projects shifted from irrigation utilization to resource management. A project was undertaken to prevent environmental degradation in the Himalayan regions of two northern states (Himachal Pradesh and Haryana).

Of special interest is the development of a portfolio of national watershed management projects. Two such projects, each covering a number of states, were funded in the late 1980s and aimed at improving yields in rain-fed areas through in situ moisture conservation practices along with vegetative bunding (vetiver grass) for slope stabilization. Another type of area development project formulated at the end of the 1980s consisted of state-specific integrated agricultural development projects containing components for irrigation, extension, various activities allied to agriculture, and elements of institution building. Yet another project is addressed to the development of a tribal area in the economically backward state of Bihar.

Regional imbalances are wide in India, there is evidence that they have worsened over time, and backward regions are an important aspect of the poverty problem. In this context it is a pity that the Bank has not been able so far to assist area-specific, broad-based rural development in India through investments, lending, and other programs for income generation, employment creation, provision of rural infrastructure, facilities to meet basic needs, and so on. India has a number of central and state-level programs in this area, and the Bank's involvement in them would have been of great value in many ways. Apart from increased funding, a fruitful dialogue might have taken place over how to improve the concepts, design, institutions, implementation, and cost-effectiveness of area development projects, with both partners benefiting from the lessons learned. These opportunities have been missed primarily because of the government's reluctance to entertain the Bank's involvement, but perhaps also because the Bank has not shown much eagerness to get into this thorny area.[49]

Rural development on an area-specific basis has been one of the Bank's continuing concerns in Bangladesh. In 1976, soon after the country was formed, a pilot loan for rural development was made drawing inspiration from the experiment undertaken in the Comilla region in the 1960s under the leadership of Akhter Hamid Khan. On the whole, project performance was not satisfactory, and the design turned out to be too complex and expensive to implement effectively. Monitoring and evaluation were not adequate to provide lessons for future lending.[50]

Further lending in this subsector has consisted of an employment-oriented project in 1980 to complete earthworks (roads and minor irrigation) undertaken in the food-for-work program, and a second and much larger ($100 million) rural development project in 1983. The latter is a countrywide project with provision for credit, irrigation, institution building, and assistance to the Bangladesh Rural Development Board. In the absence so far of audited project performance reports, it is hard to assess the impact of these projects.

Sri Lanka initiated a rural development scheme in 1979 as part of a package to balance economic liberalization with social justice and as a follow-up to an earlier decision to decentralize development efforts at the district, division, and village levels. The Bank has involved itself in this program and during 1979–83 financed three projects covering five districts. Bank projects have supported productive activities such as tree crop planting, economic infrastructure (tanks and roads), agricultural services and credit, basic needs (education, health, and water supply), and rural electrification. The first two projects (Kurunegala, started in 1979, and Matale and Puttalam, 1981) have performed well, but the third, in the northern districts (Vavuniya and Mannar, 1983), has been set back by ethnic unrest. In contrast to similar projects financed by other donors, Bank projects are implemented by line officials in Sri Lanka's administrative structure without any expatriate participation. The Bank's willingness to mesh its lending with the contents and delivery structures of an ongoing government program has been an important factor in the smooth, cost-effective, institution-strengthening implementation of these projects. The criticism has been made, however, that the Bank has been reluctant to deviate from its project blueprint, unlike sponsors of other projects, which have provided more flexibility; it is also asserted that beneficiaries under Bank projects tend to be small farmers rather than more disadvantaged groups such as landless households.[51]

TREE CROP DEVELOPMENT IN SRI LANKA. Tree crops—tea, rubber, and coconut—are vital to the Sri Lankan economy. They contribute about half of merchandise exports, with tea alone accounting for about 40 percent, and provide a significant proportion of revenues and employment. The major tea and rubber estates in Sri Lanka were nationalized in the early 1970s under land reform legislation. There has been a sharp secular decline since the early 1960s in the production and export of tree crops because of international competition, declines in export prices, poor public sector management, and excessive domestic taxation.

Since 1978 the Bank has assisted six tree crop projects. The first tree crop diversification project (1978), which aimed to diversify unsuitable estate tea lands into mixed tree crops and to resettle estate labor, was a failure largely because of intense social and political opposition, which the Bank had failed to anticipate. The other projects have been reasonably successful, despite delays and cost increases, in realizing the objectives of rehabilitation, diversification, new planting, and institutional development. To improve the profitability of the tea and rubber plantations, the Bank has engaged in a protracted dialogue with the government on the reduction of export taxes and has achieved some progress in this regard.

It is commendable that the Bank has contributed to the development of Sri Lanka's tree crop sector, overcoming its inhibition against lending for public sector enterprises. However, one criticism that has been made is that the smallholder component in the tea and smallholder rubber projects has not had much impact.[52] This is a shortcoming from the point of view of both equity and growth, because smallholders in Sri Lanka account for a third of tea, two-thirds of rubber, and almost all of coconut production.

## The Social Sectors

The share of the social sectors—education, population control, health and nutrition, urban development, and water supply and sewerage—in total Bank lending to South Asia sharply increased in the 1970s and 1980s, from barely 3 percent before 1970 to 10 to 12 percent. All Bank lending to the region for population control, nutrition, and urban development has come in these two decades. Table 10 provides data on the pattern of lending for the social sectors in South Asia over this period.

EDUCATION. Except for a small loan of $12 million for two agricultural universities, lending in the educational sector in India has consisted of two large loans for vocational training and education of technicians in 1989 ($280 million) and in 1990 ($260 million). These loans are too recent for their results to be assessed. Although the Bank has been interested in lending for general (nontechnical) education in India, the government has not been responsive.

The Bank began lending for education in Pakistan in 1964 but did not seriously involve itself in this sector until 1977, despite Pakistan's strikingly low levels of educational development. Operations in the 1960s were for small amounts, directed to vocational training. During 1977–86 three loans for general education (for a total of $77.5 million) and two for vocational training ($65.2 million) were made. Substantially larger loans for primary education were made only at the close of the 1980s: $145 million in 1987 and $112.5 million in 1990. Audited performance reports for the first three loans in Pakistan provide a largely negative picture of performance, with two of these projects being rated as unsatisfactory. Assessments are not yet available for the more recent primary education projects funded in 1984, 1987, and 1990.

In Bangladesh it took the Bank nearly a decade to make its first loan for primary education. The loan of $40 million in 1980 was, however, a substantial one. It extended to parts of eight districts and covered about 10 percent of the country. There were shortfalls in a number of project objectives, and outcome indicators relating to enrollment and dropout ratios in the project area did not indicate any clear improvement. Questions were raised about the sustainability of the project and whether the project implementation unit created for it was the appropriate institutional option.[53] Bangladesh has also received loans for vocational (including agricultural) training, technical education, and business management and civil service training. In Sri Lanka two loans have been made for training in the construction industry and a large one in 1990 ($49 million) for general education aimed at quality improvement and institutional strengthening.

Several issues concern the Bank's lending strategy in the education sector and the impact, sustainability, and replicability of Bank-financed projects. The evaluation literature, in the form of PPARs and sector studies, for South Asia is quite limited, however, because substantial lending has taken place only since the mid-1980s, and educational loans have been slow in disbursement.[54]

POPULATION. More than 95 percent of the Bank's lending in the area of population control in South Asia is concentrated in India and Bangladesh.[55] India has had a strong, well-articulated commitment to population control, especially since the mid-1960s. The Bank's first loan to India in this area was made in 1972, the year it began lending for population-related projects, but the second operation came a full eight years later, in 1980. The Bank's reluctance to be associated with population control in this interregnum may have been influenced by public reaction to forced stabilization during the emergency period (1975–77) in India.

Up to 1988 the Bank had funded five projects in all, for a total of $245.7 million; this represents a small fraction (less than 4 percent) of India's outlays on family welfare. Four of the projects were for provision of infrastructure (buildings and vehicles), staff, training, and services (such as IEC, or information, education, and communication) in selected districts of various states, and the fifth was for urban services in Bombay and Madras.

Outcome indicators in the first two projects did not reveal any improvement in contraceptive prevalence or in maternal and child health indicators in project areas over nonproject ones in the same region. Project components relating to monitoring and evaluation, operations research, and IEC have also failed to perform up to expectations. Altogether, neither the scale and continuity of the Bank's lending nor the design and impact of its projects have had much influence on India's population program in terms of policy, improvements to implementation, or lessons learned. Essentially their main contribution has been to provide infrastructural support to ongoing programs.

The Indian population program has been criticized on a number of counts, mainly the following. It is charged that there is an excessive concentration on population control, based chiefly on sterilization, to the relative neglect of maternal and child health and allied programs such as female literacy, water supply, and sanitation. Wide regional disparities in the provision and acceptance of services are also noted, with the populous, high-fertility northern Indian states faring worse than the rest. Finally, the program is criticized for excessive emphasis on the supply side and not enough on demand generation through IEC.

It is widely acknowledged that future reductions in fertility will depend largely on methods of birth spacing for younger mothers and on efforts to improve maternal and child health and female literacy, with necessary improvements in the delivery of services, including greater involvement of community and nonofficial groups. The sixth (in 1989, for $124.6 million) and seventh (in 1990, for $96.7 million) Bank-sponsored projects at the close of the 1980s addressed some of these priorities. They were also larger in loan amount and scope. The Bank has secured a foothold at the national policy level only in the seventh project. If this had happened earlier, the Bank could have gained greater leverage in this program, which in India is entirely supported by central funds.

In contrast, the Bank's involvement in population matters in Bangladesh has been much more venturesome. The first project (in 1975) was nationwide and multisectoral, involving eight different ministries and including a number of components. Subsequent projects in 1979 and in 1986 have doubled the amounts lent in previous projects and have been equally wide in scope. All these projects were cofinanced by a number of bilateral donors, who contributed considerable grant funds, thereby providing flexibility. The Bank has played a leading and catalytic role in mobilizing and coordinating foreign assistance in this field.

The main criticism of Bank projects in Bangladesh is that their magnitude, complexity, and momentum have overwhelmed the capacity of the Bangladesh government's administrative apparatus to absorb them, leading to serious shortcomings in coordination at the middle levels of administration and in quality of services in the field. However, the "big push" approach followed in Bangladesh, although wasteful, was perhaps crucial in reducing total fertility from 7 percent to below 5 percent and in increasing the prevalence of contraceptive use from 3 to 32 percent between 1970 and 1989, in a country with very low and almost stagnant levels of socioeconomic development. The Bank has recognized, however, that its future strategy in Bangladesh cannot be a mere continuation of the past: the approach will have to be intensive and fine-tuned rather than extensive and eclectic.

The Bank's only loan in Pakistan is a small one ($18 million in 1983) to support promotional efforts. Despite its great need, Pakistan has not adopted active measures for population control. After years of indecision caused mainly by political and religious opposition, the Population Welfare Plan (PWP) in Pakistan was introduced in 1980. It is a low-key, phased approach designed to promote demand for, and acceptability of, contraceptive services through maternal and child health services, functional education, and programs for women's welfare.[56] The Bank's only other loan in the population policy area was one to Sri Lanka ($17.5 million in 1988); that loan has a large health component stressing maternal and child health and birth spacing methods. It is ironic that Pakistan, with more than a threefold higher fertility rate and a six-fold larger population than Sri Lanka, has received the same amount of lending in this sector, although of course the Bank cannot be blamed for this.

NUTRITION. The Bank's interventions in nutrition have been confined to two projects in the southern state of Tamil Nadu in India. The first Tamil Nadu Integrated Nutrition Project (TINP-1) of 1980 has been adjudged a successful model of cost-effective targeting in tackling malnutrition among children in the vulnerable age group of 6 to 36 months. During the project period severe malnutrition (grades 3 and 4) in the target group has been reduced by a third to a half through selective food supplementation based on periodic weight and growth monitoring. The second project (1990) covers those districts in the state not covered in the first one and incorporates the lessons learned in it. Valuable and innovative as the project has been, its replication in other states in India is in some doubt, mainly because the Bank's highly selective approach to nutrition supplementation is politically unpalatable. The Bank has recently assisted the centrally supported Integrated Child Development Services (ICDS) program, which is less selective in its feeding program and includes preschool education as one of its components; in the process the Bank's influence has led to necessary modifications in the ICDS.

URBAN DEVELOPMENT. The Bank has given substantial support to urban projects in the major South Asian countries. A number of the principal cities in the subcontinent—Calcutta, Bombay, Madras, and Kanpur (in India), Lahore (Pakistan), Dhaka and Chittagong (Bangladesh), and Colombo (Sri Lanka)— have received urban development loans. In India the portfolio includes repeat loans to major cities such as Calcutta, Bombay, and Madras; separate loans for public (bus) transport in some of them (including Bombay and Calcutta); and projects for major towns besides the main metropolis in a number of states (Madhya Pradesh, Gujarat, Uttar Pradesh, Tamil Nadu). In 1988 the Bank also made a substantial loan ($250 million) to the Housing Development Finance Corporation, the major Indian private sector institution engaged in mortgage financing. In Sri Lanka the Bank's urban sector study of 1984 was welcomed by the government as very useful and was followed by a loan in 1986 to support a number of sectoral programs in Colombo and other urban areas.

Typically, urban projects have straddled a number of sectors and implementing agencies. The Calcutta project (1974), for instance, contained forty-four sub-projects in six sectors, and the Madras project (1977) involved ten agencies dealing with six sectors. As might be expected in such wide-ranging projects, coordination has turned out to be a major problem in the short term, while the longer-term financial and institutional sustainability of many projects is not assured. Other problems have included land acquisition delays, underfunding of local costs, and poor cost recovery, especially in the bus transport and settlement components. A valuable contribution of the Bank is the introduction of the concepts of "sites and services" and slum improvement. These have proved to be affordable, low-cost, replicable solutions to urban housing. The Bank's assistance is only a small part of what is needed to tackle urban problems in South Asia, but its contribution in demonstrating workable options has been appreciated.

WATER SUPPLY AND SEWERAGE. The Bank has been very active in the area of water supply and sewerage, largely as an adjunct to its support for urban development. It has financed major urban water supply projects in India (in Bombay, Madras, Hyderabad, and major towns in several states, including Uttar Pradesh, Maharashtra, Punjab, Rajasthan, and Tamil Nadu), Pakistan (Lahore and Karachi), Bangladesh (Dhaka and Chittagong), and Sri Lanka (Greater Colombo and other important towns). Support to rural water supply has been limited to a single project in India (in Kerala state). Many water supply and sewerage projects have encountered delays and cost overruns. In a number of cases inadequate initial investigations, design changes, and poor performance by consultants have been responsible for delays and cost escalation. By and large, however, project objectives have been achieved. Cost recovery has remained the major problem in most projects.

## The Lending Experience: A Critical Assessment

The Bank's contributions in the last two decades to economic development in South Asia have been substantial and many-sided. In nominal terms, the volume of lending in the 1970s increased to as much as four times that of the 1960s and grew threefold again in the 1980s. Resource transfers in these two decades have included a substantial element of local cost financing, providing both external and counterpart domestic resources in freely usable forms. In all South Asian countries Bank lending has played a critically important role in supplementing the foreign exchange required for development; concurrently, it has substantially supplemented domestic saving in countries where it is relatively low such as Pakistan, Bangladesh, and Nepal.

Coming predominantly in the form of project lending, the Bank's resource transfers have resulted in investments in many sectors of crucial importance to South Asia's growth, self-reliance, and welfare. As a development lender, the Bank has been interested in extending the benefits of its project lending beyond the successful completion of the project itself to improvements in implementation capacity, long-term sustainability of projects, diffusion and replication of the learning experience in project execution, institution building, and sectoral policy reforms.

This concluding section turns to a summary assessment of the impact of the principal characteristics of the Bank's project lending in South Asia, as they have emerged in actual practice in the last two decades, on the realization of the Bank's larger developmental objectives. The assessment is critical and concentrates on what the Bank could or might have done differently to realize a greater measure of success in achieving its stated objectives. This selective focus is heuristic and should not be misunderstood as partial or prejudiced: it is not meant to underestimate the Bank's considerable positive contributions, all of which have been duly noted in the earlier sections, or the considerable problems that the Bank has encountered with its South Asian borrowers.

## Lending Strategies

There can be no question that the broad lending strategies of the Bank in South Asia, in terms of sectoral and subsectoral involvement, have been appropriate to the developmental priorities and resource endowments of the borrowers in the region. Support for agriculture, with special emphasis on irrigation, agricultural credit, and extension services, along with financing of fertilizer manufacture, has reinforced the adoption of new technology that can achieve higher yields. Energy investments have been of crucial importance, and their diversification into oil, gas, and coal has helped to reduce the region's hydrocarbon imports. Lending to development financing institutions has provided a wide spectrum of support to medium-sized industries in the private sector. In the social sectors, lending for urban development, water supply, and population control have been especially worthwhile.

It can be argued that the Bank might have paid more attention to certain subsectors (small-scale enterprises, rural roads, rural water supply) than it has; that it could have involved itself earlier in some important activities (general education in Pakistan and Bangladesh, for example); and that there could have been a greater continuity in lending in some cases (in power in Sri Lanka, for example). However, one cannot come to definitive judgments on such issues because many factors—the Bank's own familiarity and comparative advantage, borrowers' preferences, and the availability and terms of other sources of finance—determine the pattern of sectoral involvement.

## Project Features

To proceed from the broad sectoral to the project level, valid criticisms of project designs and other modalities of the lending process may be raised. The very substantial increases in lending in South Asia that occurred in the 1970s and 1980s have both enabled and entailed—especially in India—relatively large loans for individual projects or for lending through intermediary institutions. Large and repeat projects have facilitated resource transfer targets, helped in institution building (for instance, the National Thermal Power Corporation and the training-and-visit approach to agricultural extension in India), and economized on transaction costs such as staff time involved in preparation, appraisal, and negotiation.

However, these projects have not been without their disadvantages. First, there have been important diseconomies of scale. Often, large projects have involved multiple components or multiple executing agencies and locations.

They have been difficult to coordinate, implement, and monitor, entailing a higher intensity of supervision. This, in turn, has reduced staff time available for preparation and appraisal, diluting their quality and exacerbating the burden on supervision. Second, large investments and repeat projects have discouraged experimentation, lesson learning, and institution building, all of which would call for a more relaxed and reflective pace of lending. Third, it has been difficult to postpone lending for large projects when that might be called for, because of the disruption it would cause to annual lending programs based on resource transfer targets. This inflexibility has reduced the Bank's leverage in the policy dialogue, as exemplified by several cases in India involving energy, agricultural credit, and irrigation.

The structural, technical, and institutional aspects of Bank projects have also come in for criticism. In India the Bank's own evaluations have wondered whether time-slice and sectoral approaches have not resulted in inadequate attention to project preparation, appraisal, and sequencing. The Bank has also been criticized for seeking to introduce uniform water management regimens in different parts of a large country like India without due regard for local conditions.[57] In Pakistan the Bank had to reverse its approach to waterlogging and salinity from SCARP-type vertical drainage relying on public tubewells to horizontal drainage and private tubewells. In Bangladesh, despite much trial and error over the years, flood control has remained intractable, and major problems connected with tubewell irrigation have remained unresolved. In Sri Lanka the Bank has had to acquiesce in the accelerated Mahaweli program instead of being able to steer its composition and phasing by optimal cost-effectiveness considerations. In agricultural extension the Bank has replicated the standard training-and-visit blueprint without taking pause to learn from experience. As the independent review of the Narmada project has shown, investigations of environmental aspects have not been timely, adequate, or thorough. Educational lending has lacked critical mass or continuity. Lending for population management in Bangladesh has involved excessive cost, both financial and institutional; in India it has concentrated too much on civil construction.

## Implementation

Implementation is primarily the responsibility of the borrower. Performance here has varied across sectors, countries, states in India, and time periods, depending on both macroeconomic and project-specific factors and subject to disruptions caused by unpredictable natural events. No data are available to assess how Bank-financed projects have fared compared with those financed by other donors or by borrowers on their own. However, interregional comparisons among the Bank's borrowers broadly indicate that project performance in South Asia was, if anything, somewhat better than the global average during most of 1970–90.

For its part, the Bank has striven through its supervisory missions to promote concern for time, cost, and quality at all stages of project execution. Considerable technical assistance has also been provided in the course of supervision. Supervision coefficients (staff weeks spent on supervision per project in a year) have been relatively high in South Asia, in part because of the high proportion of agricultural projects, which have entailed detailed monitoring and technical assistance. Other factors are the size and complexity of projects and problems arising from center-state relations in India. Furthermore, supervision intensity is explained by the fact that in complex projects not all components get prepared or appraised to the same degree of adequacy or readiness; the load on supervision in these circumstances is a reflection of "deferred preparation and appraisal."

Resident missions have been given a role in supervision, principally in agricultural projects in India and in the social sectors in Pakistan and Bangladesh. Being nearer to the field, they have been able to monitor implementation problems closely and respond to them quickly. The other side of the coin is that proximity breeds intrusiveness; resident staff have sometimes been perceived as breathing down the neck of executing agencies. But on the whole, if Indian experience is any guide, the Bank's supervision inputs have been considered helpful, and its assistance in solving field-level problems has been appreciated.[58]

Problems relating to management of projects by the borrowing country have been a matter of serious and frequent concern in project execution in South Asia. Most such deficiencies have had their roots and ramifications in country-wide problems—political, economic, and administrative. When this is the case, the lack of success in implementation reflects generic problems in the borrower's entire project portfolio. It is clear, by the same token, that better performance of the Bank's portfolio can be achieved in the longer run only by strengthening borrowers' overall institutional capabilities to prepare, execute, monitor, and supervise projects.

In principle, the Bank has been interested in strengthening such capabilities in the apex ministries and technical agencies of its borrowers, but in practice it has not invested enough effort and time in a generalized effort to strengthen project-related capacities across the board in ministries and technical agencies at the national and subnational levels. Essentially, the imperative of meeting lending targets has not allowed projects to proceed at a pace patient enough to secure a larger involvement of borrower agencies at various stages of the project cycle. (Interestingly, on the other hand, the same consideration has made the Bank quite patient with failures to comply with covenants.)

In some ways Bank projects also appear to have had negative effects on the general portfolio management of borrowers. The Bank's insistence on staffing, funding, and other specific commitments on the projects for which it lends has diverted manpower as well as material and financial resources from non-Bank-financed projects, affecting complementary investments and overall development. This has been the case particularly in staff-intensive activities (training-and-visit extension services, education, population control) and in projects entailing lumpy outlays (irrigation, urban development, water supply).

## Evaluation

Monitoring and evaluation during project execution has been a weak area. In a number of projects, appropriate mechanisms either were not put in place soon enough or did not produce useful lessons for future operations.[59] This has had especially adverse implications in projects envisaged as pilot operations, meant to provide a basis for wider replication. The contribution of ex post evaluation to operations has also been limited. In the case of repeat projects based on more or less standard blueprints, such evaluations have not been able to contribute to midcourse modifications because the pace of lending has been too fast to be steadied or steered by PCRs and PPARs finalized several years after project initiation. On the other hand, in one-of-a-kind projects, insights from PPARs have not had a wider application.

The usefulness of PPARs is further limited because they are confined to comparing results at or around the time of project completion with estimates and objectives at the time of appraisal. There are several problems in relying on economic rates of return reestimated in PCRs or PPARs as indicators of project performance. First, variations can be quite large between the initial estimates made at appraisal and those made at project completion, because of windfall increases or calamitous declines in output prices. Second, in many cases project benefits are estimated with reference to what would have obtained in the absence of the investment. This involves counterfactual judgments that may not always be reliable. Third, in some cases economic rates of return depend on assumed returns on subsystems (agricultural extension, for example), whose performance cannot be separated from that of related investments and activities (credit, irrigation) that impinge on the project but are outside of its scope. Fourth, rates of return reestimated immediately after project completion do not give any idea of what they are likely to be through the life of the project—thus they do not throw light on the sustainability of the project.

Many "new style" projects in agriculture and the social sectors, unlike the traditional ones, do not relate to fixed installations such as power plants or fertilizer factories, whose performance can be more or less guaranteed on completion, but instead entail continuing activities that are more fragile because they involve "software" and a human dimension: examples are on-farm water use and the delivery of agricultural extension, educational, population, and nutrition services. In such cases it is necessary to return to the project once a reasonable period has elapsed since its completion, to find out whether planned inputs and expected outcomes have been sustained on a durable basis. The Bank has undertaken some impact evaluations and sustainability studies of its projects, but not on a sufficient scale or on a systematic basis. This is, indeed, a serious gap.

### Policy Dialogue

In the course of financing single projects, repeat projects, and clusters of projects, the Bank's technical assistance and policy dialogue have extended upstream to issues of general application at the subsectoral and sectoral levels. There have been numerous examples. The emphasis on on-farm development and user-level water management has provided a much-needed corrective to irrigation practices in all of South Asia. The insistence on groundwater discipline, dam safety, and resettlement and rehabilitation of displaced families has focused attention on important issues that tend to be neglected.

Despite its continuing problems, the training-and-visit approach represents a major contribution to the reform of agricultural administration. Project designs in India for watershed management and nutrition have been innovative. Tree crop projects in Sri Lanka have enabled the Bank to secure changes in export taxes. Financing of fertilizer projects has provided a nexus for price reform in Pakistan and Bangladesh. General-purpose lending through DFIs has been better focused. Energy conservation and productivity improvements have been promoted in refineries, fertilizer plants, power plants, and the cement industry. Technology has been modernized in railways and telecommunications. Needless to say, the Bank has not been successful in all that it has attempted, but it has succeeded in charting initiatives of much relevance for its borrowers.

By and large, the Bank's efforts to enforce financial covenants of various kinds—relating to cost recovery, tariffs, self-financing, receivables, and repayments—have not been successful. In India and Sri Lanka, which have continued to hold regular elections, populist politics has been a serious obstacle to liberalizing tariffs, reducing subsidies, and ensuring loan repayments, even to the extent to which governments have been interested in doing these things. Basically, it has not been possible for the Bank to gain enough leverage on such issues at the sectoral level from individual project operations, however large and continuous they have been. Ironically, in fact, the size and continuity of lending operations have blunted the pressure for reform.

In practical terms, the only option available to the Bank has been the "exit" option—to discontinue lending pending the demonstration of serious intent for reforms. Indeed, that is the option that the Bank has taken, later rather than sooner, in the cases of NABARD and NTPC in India, for example. In Pakistan and Bangladesh as well, it has not always been easy to enforce financial and revenue covenants, although the situation has been somewhat more encouraging than in India: cost recovery in irrigation, power, and gas steadily improved in the 1980s, and progress has been made in fertilizer pricing reform. Adjustment lending in Pakistan and Bangladesh has no doubt been a factor in inducing progress in these directions.

The Bank's policy dialogue has not been confined to the project or to project-related sectors. Annual country economic memorandums (CEMs), sector- and issue-related studies prepared as part of CEMs, and other economic and sectoral studies have all provided opportunities for the Bank to interact with borrowers at the policy level and with line ministries and executing agencies. They have also provided an agenda for lending operations, especially for adjustment lending. In the 1980s the Bank issued a number of economic and sectoral reviews of high quality.[60]

There has not, however, been much sharing of the Bank's policy analyses and prescriptions with the media, nongovernmental organizations, and academia as part of a wider effort to mold opinion among the public at large, even in a country like India which offers good opportunities for doing so. Bank studies more often get leaked than published, with the consequence that the Bank tends to be characterized as an agent of external pressure rather than as a partner in development. In good measure, borrower governments are responsible for creating a conspiratorial ambience around the policy dialogue between them and the Bank; in doing so they have only added to their own problems in securing understanding and support in the public domain for reforms.

Within governments, the Bank's policy interaction has been closest with ministries of finance and relatively less with planning commissions, line ministries, and technical agencies. Ministries of finance have tended to centralize the aid relationship and have been reluctant to allow Bank staff to "run around." On the other hand, sector ministries, apex agencies, and state and provincial governments in India and Pakistan, lacking direct interest in aid mobilization, have not been eager to entertain criticism of their policies and programs. Nevertheless, acting mainly at the operational level, resident missions have made a quiet contribution over time to interpreting the Bank to the borrowers and vice versa. In this background, the advice that there is a need for "more, more expert, more senior, more continuous, more project-localized Bank expertise" in resident missions is well taken.[61]

### Institution Building

The institutional aspects of the policy dialogue require discussion at different levels. At the project level the Bank has faced the familiar dilemma between devising ad hoc structures for implementing its projects and strengthening existing institutions. Ad hoc institutional innovations have had a mixed record in terms of their effectiveness and sustainability. In many urban projects they have been useful; however, in training-and-visit they have encountered serious difficulties, and the project implementation units in the Bangladesh educational and population programs have not proved appropriate. In South Asia the Bank's recourse to such "island" models has, however, been limited. By and large, the Bank has wisely opted to strengthen existing institutions in its lending operations.

Another aspect of institutional interaction relates to the public sector. In the late 1960s, when the Bank overcame its unwillingness to lend to public sector enterprises, the breakthrough had particularly beneficial results in South Asia by enabling substantial investments in oil, gas, and coal throughout most of the region; in fertilizer manufacture in India, Pakistan and Bangladesh; and in the tree crop sector in Sri Lanka. These major exceptions apart, the Bank has not been able to shed its inhibition toward public ownership at the ideological or at the practical level. Periods of nationalization in Pakistan, Bangladesh, and Sri Lanka have met with a contraction in the Bank's overall lending, and not just for industry. In India, although a Bank study of the steel sector identified opportunities for lending for rehabilitation and improvement, the Bank finally decided not to proceed.[62] In many situations, particularly in India and Sri Lanka, the Bank has tended to ignore chances to lend to state enterprises and has missed opportunities for improving their performance by getting involved. (Ironically, on the other hand, the Bank has at times stayed with the public sector long after objective factors ceased to justify doing so, tubewell irrigation in Pakistan and Bangladesh being a major example.)

Institution building, from a broader perspective, also involves strengthening domestic capabilities outside the state sector. Features of the Bank's lending such as local cost financing, domestic price preference in international competitive bidding, and earmarked local bidding have made a definite contribution in this respect. However, the Bank's use of consultants—on its own account for project preparation, appraisal, and supervision—has tended to favor expatriates in preference to domestic consultants. This has not only conflicted with the need to develop the good potential for domestic consulting expertise in major South Asian countries but has also adversely affected project performance, in some cases because of a lack of continuity (and perhaps also of commitment) in exogenous advice. For their part, South Asian governments themselves have not done enough to utilize or encourage their domestic consultancy resources.

The Bank has given substantial assistance to intermediaries such as NABARD, the National Cooperative Development Corporation (NCDC), and the Indian Dairy Corporation (IDC) in India, and BADC in Bangladesh. Its loans to the Indian Farmers Fertilizers Cooperative have provided valuable support to the cooperative sector in India's fertilizer industry. Many components in the Bank's urban development and water supply projects have been implemented through urban local authorities, and rural development projects in Sri Lanka have utilized decentralized entities with good success. However, despite many opportunities for doing so, the Bank has not ventured to work through rural local (*panchayati raj*) authorities in India. This has been both a cause and a consequence of the Bank's limited involvement in India in area development, rural roads, and rural water supply. Despite their presence in many fields of development—particularly in India, Bangladesh, and Sri Lanka—the Bank's active involvement with nongovernmental organizations has been relatively recent.

### Alleviation of Poverty

Since the 1970s poverty alleviation has been a major objective of the Bank's lending operations, besides being the subject of a great deal of its rhetoric. In the 1970s the thrust of the Bank's policy was to target urban and agricultural (especially rural development) projects to poverty groups in terms of quantified proportions of outlays or benefits. In the early 1980s the focus was widened to countrywide programming for poverty reduction.[63]

To what extent poverty alleviation has taken place at all in recent decades in major South Asian countries remains a topic of inconclusive debate. What is indisputable is that South Asian poverty is massive and deeply rooted in several structural factors. It is clearly impossible to assess at a macroeconomic level the Bank's contribution to poverty alleviation in South Asia, except to say that given the nature and dimensions of the problem, the impact of aid from all sources, let alone from the Bank, is likely to have been only marginal. This is especially the case since aid has operated through discrete projects and programs and has not addressed itself, directly or through policy dialogue, to structural changes such as land reform. We can therefore only discuss to what extent and in what ways the Bank has attempted to orient its projects toward helping the poor, and review the evidence on the success or failure of such efforts.

The Bank's agricultural portfolio can claim to be poverty-oriented in three ways: by contributing to increases in output, lending for agriculture has indirectly benefited the poor; there has been an effort to skew direct benefits to landholders toward smaller farmers; and subsectors where lending can directly benefit the landless poor (such as dairying) have been supported.

The Bank itself has not undertaken benchmark-cum-impact studies to assess the indirect (or "trickle-down") effects that its production-oriented projects may have had on sustained poverty reduction where they have been implemented. In irrigation, the emphasis at the project design stage has been on benefiting a substantial proportion of small farmers, but in practice it has been impossible to ensure any such earmarking of water use. All that has been possible is to promote greater equity among farmers—whether large, medium-size, or small—in different reaches of canal irrigation. In agricultural credit, Bank projects have attempted to channel progressively larger proportions of loans to small farmers, but this has not altered the fact that tubewells in most parts of India, Pakistan, and Bangladesh are predominantly owned by large farmers. Tractors provided through agricultural credits in Pakistan have not only favored larger farmers but have displaced employment for the rural poor. Extension projects emphasize reaching out to small farmers, but it is difficult to ensure that this is being done—the farmers contacted first by training-and-visit programs have often been the larger and more influential ones, who enjoy better access to complementary inputs such as water, credit, and fertilizers.

In the dairy cooperatives, which the Bank has substantially supported in India through the IDC, available evidence indicates that the beneficiaries have been mainly medium-size farmers rather than small farmers or landless peasants.

The social forestry projects have not, contrary to original expectations, provided the village poor with fuelwood and may have even reduced their access to traditional grazing and fuel from village commons. Bank projects in tree crop agriculture in Sri Lanka have not paid sufficient attention to smallholder plantations in rubber or tea. Broad-based rural development through area projects has been successful in Sri Lanka, but even there benefits have not percolated down to the most disadvantaged segments of the rural population. Early efforts at rural development in Bangladesh have not been a success, and the recent countrywide project has yet to show results. In India the Bank has not been able or willing to get involved in the government's antipoverty programs, such as those for drought-prone area development, asset distribution to poor rural households, and employment generation for rural unskilled labor.

In sum, it may not be unfair to conclude that thus far the Bank's contributions to poverty alleviation through its agricultural and area development operations have been neither significant nor particularly successful. Certainly, they have fallen far short of an "assault on poverty."[64]

This leaves out population, nutrition, education, urban, and water supply projects, which include several elements of poverty alleviation. In Bangladesh the Bank's population programs have aided the decline in fertility. The emphasis on rural, primary, and girls' education in Pakistan and Bangladesh has been useful, but neither the continuity and scale of Bank assistance to general education nor project performance has been such as to make any tangible impact. The nutrition project in India has demonstrated a cost-effective approach for tackling malnourishment in children, to which those of the poor are most exposed, but it has been confined so far to parts of a single state. The settlement and water supply projects have undoubtedly benefited the poorer, although not the poorest, sections of urban and semiurban populations in a number of major cities and towns.

By the beginning of the 1990s the Bank had once again reformulated its approach to poverty reduction. "Sustainable poverty reduction" has been described as "the Bank's overarching objective." The new, two-pronged strategy relies, on the one hand, on economic growth to generate income-earning opportunities for the poor, and, on the other, improved access to education, health care, and other social services to help the poor take advantage of these opportunities. The consequent core poverty lending program (1990–93) envisages a number of projects in India, Pakistan, Bangladesh, and Sri Lanka that will seek to translate this strategy into lending operations.[65]

## Conclusion

One cannot but conclude that, in actual practice, the Bank's project lending in South Asia has fallen short of the expectations, and often the claims, placed on it by the Bank. Although, to be sure, several factors relating to the borrowers are responsible for this outcome, the Bank's own actions have contributed to less-than-optimal benefits from project lending. Three interrelated approaches predominate.

First, resource transfer considerations—however valid in their own right—have had an adverse impact on various stages of the project cycle. Based on balance of payments needs on the demand side and lending targets on the supply side—arrived at annually in meetings of consortia and consultative groups—the Bank has proceeded to program its project operations, subjecting them to tightly administered lending schedules. Targeted lending of this kind has had wide-ranging implications for lending strategies, project preparation, appraisal, implementation and supervision, and the policy dialogue.

Second, the Bank has followed what might be called an incremental strategy in the pursuit of its policy dialogue. Basically, this strategy would appear to have been impelled by three concerns: the Bank's desire to adhere to its lending targets, its reluctance to jeopardize its relationships with its large and important South Asian borrowers, and its desire to maintain the continuity of its involvement in priority sectors of their development. In the circumstances that have prevailed in South Asia in the last two decades, this strategy of continued lending linked to promises rather than performance has had its inevitable consequences. The enforcement of basic covenants, whether related to financial performance, environmental standards, or institutional reform, has had to be soft-pedaled. Lending has had to proceed despite clear indications of systemic sectoral problems. In several cases where reforms continued to be postponed, problems eventually accumulated to a point where the Bank was forced to suspend operations, making it all the more difficult to secure them as a basis for the subsequent resumption of lending. Given these contradictions, inherent in any attempt to reconcile resource transfer targets with project-mediated developmental objectives, the only other logically valid option would have been to strike a better balance between project and nonproject lending, so that the burden on projects for resource transfers could be eased. This would have allowed the pace and pattern of project lending to be better tuned to the realization of the Bank's objectives. Concurrently, a greater measure of nonproject lending might have been able to stimulate and support reforms, so as to render project lending more efficacious.

This brings us to the third factor, which is that the Bank attempted to blend project and nonproject lending in some sort of orchestrated fashion only toward the end of the period covered in this account. Earlier, in the mid-1960s, program lending to India, while providing much-needed balance of payments support, had been aimed at persuading India to devalue, liberalize imports, and give higher priority to agriculture.[66] Program credits for industrial imports continued until the mid-1970s as a measure of support for fuller utilization of capacity. From then until 1991, when India received its first structural adjustment loan, all lending to India was through projects.

In Pakistan, program loans between the mid-1960s and the mid-1970s were basically general-purpose lending for industrial imports, without being tuned in any very specific manner to promoting or supporting macroeconomic reforms. Lending to Pakistan in nonproject form was revived only with the structural adjustment loan of 1982, the first such lending in South Asia. This was followed by sectoral adjustment lending later in the 1980s.

Program lending to Bangladesh has continued steadily since the beginning of operations in 1971 on the ground that the very difficult conditions of economic management in that country justified flexible, fast-disbursing balance of payments and budgetary support to sustain minimum levels of essential imports and to generate counterpart funds for development. The Bank's evaluation of the entire series of program credits until 1986 to Bangladesh was that they did not succeed in achieving adequate or sustained reforms at the macroeconomic or the sectoral level.[67] With this experience, the Bank has turned to sectoral adjustment lending in Bangladesh since 1987. Both Sri Lanka and Nepal received structural adjustment loans at the end of the 1980s (1990 in Sri Lanka and 1987 and 1989 in Nepal); until then there had been only one small program loan for Sri Lanka and none at all for Nepal.

Thus, in the 1960s and 1970s, the use of program lending as an instrument of policy dialogue was fitful and not particularly effective; no deliberate attempt was made until the adjustment loans, mostly in the late 1980s, to coordinate nonproject and project lending with further macroeconomic and sectoral reforms. The fact that, effectively, project lending has been the only available mode for the policy dialogue—entirely so in India and for the most part in other South Asian countries—has meant that several objectives of the Bank as a development lender have had to be pursued through a single instrumentality. The result has been that achievement of these objectives has been less than optimal.

The 1990s may well prove to be a watershed in terms of both the quantum and the nature of the Bank's lending operations in South Asia. In varying degrees, all South Asian borrowers will remain dependent on aid in the proximate future, and within the Bank Group they will be critically dependent on lending from the International Development Association (IDA). It has been possible to compensate for the decline in South Asia's share in IDA resources in the 1980s through substantial increases in IBRD lending to India and Pakistan. In the 1990s the current attenuated creditworthiness of India and Pakistan will not permit anything like the increment in Bank loans that occurred in the previous decade. Objectively, a strong case can be made for increasing IDA allocations to South Asia, particularly to India.[68] However, there is no escaping the fact that IDA resources will continue to be scarce because of the pressure on them from sub-Saharan Africa and from new Central Asian borrowers. In this context, efficiency in resource use rather than ready resource transfers will have to be the dominant note of lending operations. Alongside and related to this is the phase of Bank-supported adjustment—macroeconomic and sectoral—in which all South Asian countries, including India, now find themselves. This will entail a much larger share in total lending (increasing at a slower pace) for nonproject adjustment lending, leaving fewer resources for project lending. The major challenge that the Bank and its borrowers will face in these circumstances will be, on the one hand, to get much more out of project lending in terms of execution and impact and, on the other, to deploy adjustment lending for macroeconomic and sectoral reforms that can maximize the effectiveness of discrete project investments. The decade ahead is thus likely to be both lean and hard for the Bank and its borrowers in South Asia.

# Notes

1. South Asia, for the purposes of this paper, includes India, Pakistan, Bangladesh, Sri Lanka, Nepal, Bhutan, and Maldives. The Bank's classification of South Asia has reflected, over the years, growth in its membership and changes consequent on internal administrative reorganizations. India was an original signatory to the Bretton Woods agreements. Pakistan joined the Bank in 1950, to be followed by Sri Lanka (then Ceylon) in the same year. Nepal became a member in 1961. These four countries along with Afghanistan, Iran, and Burma constituted the Bank's "South Asia" before 1973. The region was merged into "Asia" during 1973–75, when Bangladesh joined the Bank (1973) upon its emergence as a separate country. Between 1975 and 1987, when South Asia again came to be treated as a separate region, it included India, Pakistan, Bangladesh, Myanmar, Nepal, Sri Lanka, Maldives (which became a member in 1978), and Bhutan (in 1981). In the reorganization of the Bank in 1987, Pakistan was included in the Europe, Middle East, and North Africa (EMENA) region, and the other seven countries were merged in Asia. The reorganization of 1991 revived South Asia as a separate region comprising the seven countries covered in this chapter.

2. Except where the International Bank for Reconstruction and Development (IBRD) and the International Development Association (IDA) are distinguished in the text or in context, references to "the Bank" include IDA, and loan amounts include credits.

3. The growth rates given here are official U.S. dollar–denominated GNP growth rates as reported by the World Bank; that is, they are generally official national estimates converted to real dollars at official exchange rates. For growth rates in the colonial period see A. Heston, "National Income," in Dharma Kumar, ed., *The Cambridge Economic History of India*, vol. 2 (Cambridge University Press, 1983), pp. 376–462.

4. There is a large literature on rural poverty in South Asia. T. N. Srinivasan and Pranab K. Bardhan, eds., *Rural Poverty in South Asia* (Columbia University Press, 1988); and Inderjit Singh, *The Great Ascent: The Rural Poor in South Asia* (Johns Hopkins University Press, 1990) are two recent contributions.

5. On regional cooperation possibilities in South Asia see B. G. Verghese, *Waters of Hope: Integrated Water Resource Development and Regional Cooperation within the Himalayan-Ganga-Brahmaputra-Barak Basin* (New Delhi: Oxford University Press and IBH Publishing House, 1990); and A. A. Waqif, ed., *Regional Cooperation in Industry and Energy: Prospects for South Asia* (New Delhi: Sage Publications, 1991). A number of studies relating to possibilities for regional cooperation have been undertaken for and under the auspices of the South Asian Association for Regional Cooperation (SAARC).

6. All figures for lending refer to initial commitments at the time of approval. They do not take into account cancellations or loans and credits not declared effective.

7. India's share in IDA lending has declined steeply from 45 percent in the 1960s to 39.5 percent in the 1970s and 23 percent in the 1980s. In recent IDA replenishments a ceiling of 30 percent has been placed on lending to India and China combined.

8. See World Bank, *World Bank in Pakistan—Review of a Relationship 1960–1984* (2 vols.), Operations Evaluation Department (OED) report 6048 (Washington, January 1986), vol. 1, pp. 12–17.

9. The early years of Bank-Bangladesh relationships are the subject of Just Faaland, ed., *Aid and Influence: The Case of Bangladesh* (St. Martin's Press, 1981).

10. See World Bank, *The World Bank and Sri Lanka: A Review of a Relationship*, OED report 6074 (Washington, 1986); see also Edward S. Mason and Robert E. Asher, *The World Bank since Bretton Woods* (Brookings, 1973), pp. 438–41.

11. These figures are based on data compiled from the Bank's annual reports.

12. This is brought out by various indicators of performance in issues of the Bank's *Annual Reviews of Project Implementation and Supervision* (ARIS).

13. Managerial problems include staffing, land acquisition, contractual, and procurement problems; in the main, financial problems relate to compliance with financial covenants and underfunding of domestic resources; political problems are identified as those arising from policy differences between the Bank and the borrower.

14. This section relies on extensive material generated by the OED, especially its project performance audit reports. Out of 530 projects funded in South Asia in the 1971–90 period, PPARs are available for 156—a reasonable sample size. In addition, country economic memorandums, country studies, sector studies, and country-specific sector studies have been useful. Independent academic studies have been valuable in supplying the pinch of salt to be taken with these Bank documents; we cite in particular the two excellent "relationship" studies dealing with Pakistan and Sri Lanka, undertaken for the OED by academic teams led by John Lewis and Gustav Papanek, respectively. In this category also belongs R. H. Cassen and others, *The Effectiveness of Aid to Pakistan: A Report to UNDP/Government of Pakistan* (Oxford: International Development Centre, 1990).

15. For a detailed account see World Bank, *A Review of World Bank Lending for Natural Gas: Country Case Study: Pakistan* , OED report 10828, June 30, 1992.

16. See World Bank, *A Review of World Bank Lending for Electric Power,* World Bank Energy Series Paper 2 (March 1988).

17. In fiscal 1990 the combined return on net assets of SEBs in India was negative, on the order of -10 percent; their operating losses exceeded the equivalent of $1.6 billion; financial subsidies were estimated at $1.9 billion, and economic subsidies were perhaps about four times as much, because average tariffs were only about 50 percent of long-run marginal costs. See World Bank, *India: Long Term Issues in the Power Sector*, report 9786-IN (1991).

18. For an account of the Bank's intervention in this phase see Mason and Asher, *The World Bank since Bretton Woods*, pp. 437–38.

19. The Bank's estimate is that the power sector alone in South Asia will need about $70 billion in foreign exchange in the 1990s, which is nearly six times the Bank's total lending for power up to fiscal 1990. See Edwin A. Moore and George Smith, *Capital Expenditure for Electric Power in the Developing Countries in the 1990s*, World Bank Energy Series Paper 21 (February 1990), p. 63.

20. World Bank, *India: Railway Modernization and Maintenance Project* (Credit 844-N), Project Performance Audit Report 7020, (November 30, 1987).

21. Alice Galenson and Louis Thompson, "The Bank's Evolving Policy Toward Railway Lending," World Bank, Infrastructure and Urban Development Department, August 1991, p. 5.

22. The loan for the public sector Thal Vaishet Fertilizer project (1979, $250 million), included in these figures, never became effective. This project is discussed later in the text.

23. World Bank, *Sustainability of Projects: Review of Experience in the Fertilizer Subsector*, OED Report 6073 (1986).

24. This and other contracts to Snamprogetti have come in for considerable criticism in India, where it is alleged that the contracts were granted as favors to the local representative of the firm, a family friend of the late Prime Minister Rajiv Gandhi.

25. World Bank, *India: Fertilizer Industry Strategy Study*, Report 6805-IN (1987).

26. The ICICI was founded in 1955 in the private sector with the active involvement of the Bank. It came under government ownership (52 percent) in 1969 after the major commercial banks, which were its shareholders, were nationalized.

27. World Bank, *India: Industrial Credit and Investment Corporation of India, Limited (Loans 789-IN and 902-IN)*, Project Performance Audit Report 3428 (April 1981), p. iv.

28. World Bank, *Bangladesh: Bangladesh Shilpa Bank (BSB) (Credit 632-BD)*, Project Performance Audit Report 6413 (September 24, 1986), p. vi.

29. World Bank, *India: Irrigation Sector Review*, 2 vols., report 9518-IN (December 20, 1991); see also World Bank, *India: 1991 Country Economic Memorandum*, vol. 2, "Agriculture, Challenges and Opportunities," report 9412-IN (August 23, 1991), pp. 74–83, 99–101.

30. See World Bank, Project Performance Audit Report 9716 (June 1991).

31. Quoted in *Sardar Sarovar: Report of the Independent Review* (Ottawa: Resource Futures International, 1992), p. 53.

32. The Sardar Sarovar dam on the Narmada River and its 75,000 kilometers of canals are intended to irrigate 1.8 million hectares, provide drinking water to 40 million people, and to generate electricity. Ibid., pp. 5, 242.

33. Memorandum from the president to the executive directors of the Bank on *India: Sardar Sarovar (Narmada) Projects*, R92-168 (September 11, 1992), p. 2.

34. World Bank, *World Bank Lending Conditionality: A Review of Cost Recovery in Irrigation Projects*, OED report 6283 (June 25, 1986), p. i.

35. For a summary of the Bank's contribution to the Indus Waters Treaty see Mason and Asher, *The World Bank since Bretton Woods*, pp. 610–27; N. D. Gulhati, *Indus Waters Treaty: An Exercise in International Mediation* (New Delhi: Allied Publishers, 1973) provides a more detailed account.

36. The framework for the Bank's activities in this phase was provided by P. Lieftinck, A. R. Sadove, and T. C. Creyke, *Water and Power Resources of West Pakistan: A Study in Sector Planning* (Johns Hopkins University Press, 1968). Canal flows in Pakistan have led to so much seepage that the water table has risen alarmingly over the years in areas without adequate drainage. This is compounded by salinity affecting 15 to 40 percent of canal command areas during various parts of the year.

37. World Bank, *World Bank in Pakistan*, vol. 2, p. 67.

38. For concise summaries see World Bank, *Bangladesh: Drainage and Flood Control Project (Credit 864-BD)*, Project Performance Audit Report 8805 (June 29, 1990), and World Bank, *Bangladesh: Promoting Higher Growth and Human Development* (Country Study, 1987), pp. 54–57.

39. World Bank, *Bangladesh: Review of the Experience with Policy Reforms in the 1980s*, OED report 8874 (1990), pp. 41–75.

40. *Ibid.*, pp. 57–80; B. Hartmann and J. K. Boyce, *Quiet Violence: A View from a Bangladesh Village* (London: Oxford University Press, 1983), chap. 19.

41. Verghese, *Waters of Hope*; and the USAID study on Eastern Waters.

42. On the Mahaweli project see World Bank, *The World Bank and Sri Lanka*, pp. 89–96; and World Bank, *Sri Lanka: A Break with the Past: The 1987–90 Program of Economic Reforms and Adjustment*, 2 vols., Report 7220-CE (May 27, 1988), vol. 2, pp. 74–88. In subsequent years expenditures on the Mahaweli project declined substantially; the major problem that remains is to reduce the large institutional structure created for it.

43. World Bank, *Agricultural Credit Projects: A Review of Recent Experience in India*, report 3415 (1981); also M. Lipton and J. Toye, *Does Aid Work in India? A Country Study of the Impact of Official Development Assistance* (London: Routledge, 1990), pp. 170–73.

44. World Bank, *India: Fourth Agricultural Refinance and Development Corporation Credit Project (ARDC IV)(Loan 2095-IN/Credit 1209-IN)*, Project Performance Audit Report 7925 (June 30, 1989), p. vi. The Bank's OED had this to say four years later about the 1986 loan to NABARD: "Since the project, starting in 1986, did not achieve significantly better results than its predecessor . . . and since the recommendations of the study team, released in 1989, have still to be implemented, the whole decision process leading up to loan approval is viewed by the Bank in retrospect to have been misguided and controlled by disbursement pressures rather than common sense." *Review of Bank Lending for Agricultural Credit and Rural Finance (1948–1992)*, report 12143 (World Bank, 1993), p. 85, para. 6.13.

45. See World Bank, *Operations Evaluation Report: Agricultural Credit Programs*, (1976); Hans P. Binswanger, *The Economics of Tractors in South Asia: An Analytic Review* (New York: Agricultural Development Council, 1978); Bina Agarwal, "Tractorisation, Productivity and Employment, A Reassessment," *Journal of Development Studies*, vol. 16 (April 1980), pp. 375–86.

46. John P. McInerney and Graham F. Donaldson, *The Consequences of Farm Tractors in Pakistan*, Working Paper 210 (World Bank, February 1975); *Operations Evaluation Report: Agricultural Credit Programs*, vol. 2, pp. 53–55; Godfrey J. Tyler, "Poverty, Income Distribution and the Analysis of Agricultural Projects," *International Labour Review*, vol. 118 (July–August 1979), pp. 459–72.

47. The T&V approach is to appoint full-time village extension workers (VEWs) to work exclusively on extension; establish a single line of command between VEWs and extension headquarters; select contact farmers to disseminate information; establish a fixed and regular cycle of fortnightly visits by VEWs; use simple, practical, relevant messages concentrating on the most important crops; provide regular in-service training to staff at all levels; initiate a system of feedback from farmers via extension staff to

researchers; and develop monitoring and evaluation procedures.

48. See National Institute of Rural Development (NIRD), *Training and Visit System of Agricultural Extension: The Indian Experience* (Hyderabad, 1983); Mick Moore "Institutional Development, The World Bank, and India's New Agricultural Extension Programme," *Journal of Development Studies*, vol. 20 (July 1984), pp. 303–17; Gershon Feder and Roger Slade, "A Comparative Analysis of Some Aspects of Training and Visit System of Agricultural Extension in India," *Journal of Development Studies*, vol. 22 (January 1986), pp. 407–27; World Bank, *India: Agricultural Extension Sector Review Report*, report 9383-IN (1988); M. Macklin, "Agriculture Extension in India: Past, Present and Future" (World Bank, 1991).

49. At the analytical level, however, the Bank has been interested in antipoverty and rural employment programs. See Robert V. Pulley, *Making the Poor Creditworthy: A Case Study of the Integrated Rural Development Program in India,* Discussion Paper 58 (World Bank, 1989); Martin Ravallion, "Reaching the Rural Poor through Public Employment: Arguments, Evidence, and Lessons from South Asia," *World Bank Research Observer*, vol. 6 (July 1991), pp. 153–75.

50. World Bank, *Bangladesh,* Project Performance Audit Report 6521 (November 1986); Michael Bamberger and Shabbir Cheema, *Case Studies of Project Sustainability: Implications for Policy and Operations from Asian Experience* (World Bank, Economic Development Institute, 1990), pp. 47–62.

51. World Bank, *Rural Development: World Bank Experience 1965–86* (1988), pp. 72–74, profile 3.

52. World Bank, *The World Bank and Sri Lanka*, p. 82.

53. Bamberger and Cheema, *Case Studies of Project Sustainability*, chap. 4.

54. The OED sector study of educational projects predates the main period of lending for education in South Asia. World Bank, *Review of Bank Operations in the Education Sector*, OED report 2321 (December 29, 1978).

55. For assessments of Bank lending for population management in India and Bangladesh see World Bank, *Population and the World Bank: A Review of Activities and Impacts from Eight Case Studies*, OED report 10021 (October 22, 1991) pp. 12–33.

56. On the evolution of population policy in Pakistan see Samuel S. Lieberman, "Accommodation and Control of Population Growth," in Shahid Javed Burki and Robert Laporte Jr., eds., *Pakistan's Development Priorities: Choices for the Future* (Oxford University Press, 1984), pp. 139–200.

57. Robert Chambers, *Managing Canal Irrigation: Practical Analysis from South Asia* (Cambridge University Press, 1988); and Robert Wade, "The World Bank and India's Irrigation Reform," *Journal of Development Studies*, vol. 18 (January 1982), pp. 171–84.

58. On the Indian experience see S. Guhan and A. Mozoomdar, *Bank Project Supervision Activities in India* (World Bank, Consultants' Report, 1989).

59. Vigar Ahmed and Michael Bamberger, *Monitoring and Evaluating Development Projects: The South Asian Experience* (World Bank, EDI, 1989).

60. These include studies relating to the agricultural sector as a whole in India, Pakistan, and Nepal; to irrigation, flood control, and drainage in India, Pakistan, and Bangladesh; and to a number of agricultural subsectors in India.

61. Lipton and Toye, *Does Aid Work in India?* p. 99.

62. *India: Steel Sector Strategy Report*, report 6599-IN (World Bank, July 1987).

63. See "Poverty Monitoring and Progress Reports," in *Poverty Reduction Handbook* (World Bank, 1992), chapter 9–I.

64. For independent assessments see Graham Donaldson, "Government-Sponsored Rural Development: Experience of the World Bank," in C. Peter Timmer, ed., *Agriculture and the State, Growth, Employment and Poverty in Developing Countries* (Cornell University Press, 1991), pp. 156–90; S. Guhan, "Aid for the Poor: Performance and Possibilities in India," in John P. Lewis, ed., *Strengthening the Poor: What Have We Learned?* (New Brunswick, Transaction Books, 1988); Hartmann and Boyce, *Quiet Violence;* and Lipton and Toye, *Does Aid Work in India?*

65. See World Bank, *World Development Report 1990: Poverty Reduction and World Bank Operations*, report 8491 (1990); and *Poverty Reduction Handbook.*

66. This phase has been described by Mason and Asher, *The World Bank since Bretton Woods*, pp. 677–83, as "the Bank's most significant attempt to use the leverage of its lending to modify macroeconomic policies in a major member country." See also John P. Lewis, *Governance and Reform: Essays in Indian Political Economy* (Oxford University Press, forthcoming).

67. World Bank, *Bangladesh: Review of the Experience,* points out that external assistance "by providing a cushion inadvertently created a desensitizing effect on the recipient's behaviour by alleviating the pressure on the political authorities to be more resolute in addressing pressing economic problems," (p. x).

68. See Robert Cassen, Vijay Joshi, and Michael Lipton, "Stabilization, Structural Reform and IDA Assistance to India" (1992).